INTRODUCING
Media Studies

Ziauddin Sardar and Borin Van Loon

Edited by Richard Appignanesi

ICON BOOKS UK   TOTEM BOOKS USA

Published in the United Kingdom
in 2000 by Icon Books Ltd.,
Grange Road, Duxford,
Cambridge CB2 4QF
e-mail: info@iconbooks.co.uk
www.iconbooks.co.uk

Published in the United States
in 2000 by Totem Books
Inquiries to: Icon Books Ltd.,
Grange Road, Duxford,
Cambridge CB2 4QF, UK
e-mail: info@iconbooks.co.uk
www.iconbooks.co.uk

Sold in the UK, Europe, South Africa
and Asia by Faber and Faber Ltd.,
3 Queen Square, London WC1N 3AU
or their agents

In the United States,
distributed to the trade by
National Book Network Inc.,
4720 Boston Way, Lanham,
Maryland 20706

Distributed in the UK, Europe,
South Africa and Asia by
Macmillan Distribution Ltd.,
Houndmills, Basingstoke RG21 6XS

Distributed in Canada by
Penguin Books Canada,
10 Alcorn Avenue, Suite 300,
Toronto, Ontario M4V 3B2

Published in Australia
in 2000 by Allen & Unwin Pty. Ltd.,
PO Box 8500, 83 Alexander Street,
Crows Nest, NSW 2065

ISBN 1 84046 114 4

Reprinted 2002

Originating editor: Richard Appignanesi

Printed and bound in Australia
by McPherson's Printing Group, Victoria

Why should we study the Media?

Television channels – terrestrial,
satellite and digital – and countless radio stations are clogging up the airwaves. Newspapers, magazines, books, comics, films, videos and animation are competing for our precious time. Advertising is almost impossible to escape. Surfing the Web is now a daily chore for most of us living in the industrialized world.

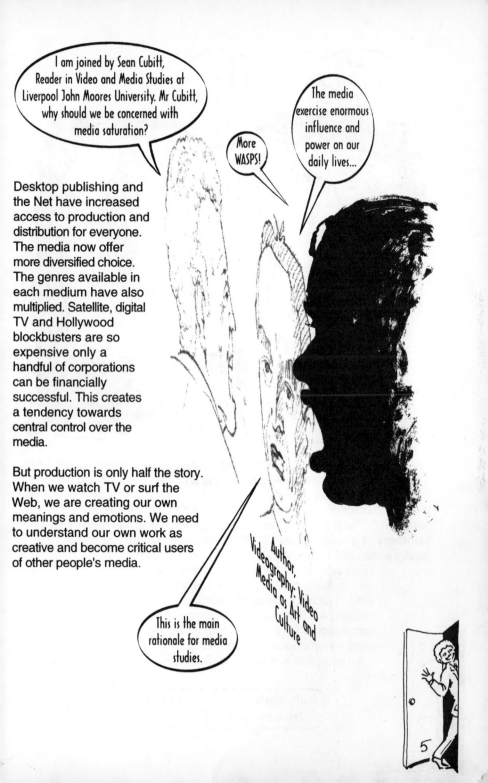

I am joined by Sean Cubitt, Reader in Video and Media Studies at Liverpool John Moores University. Mr Cubitt, why should we be concerned with media saturation?

More WASPS!

The media exercise enormous influence and power on our daily lives...

Desktop publishing and the Net have increased access to production and distribution for everyone. The media now offer more diversified choice. The genres available in each medium have also multiplied. Satellite, digital TV and Hollywood blockbusters are so expensive only a handful of corporations can be financially successful. This creates a tendency towards central control over the media.

But production is only half the story. When we watch TV or surf the Web, we are creating our own meanings and emotions. We need to understand our own work as creative and become critical users of other people's media.

This is the main rationale for media studies.

Author, Videography: Video Media as Art and Culture

5

The media mediate. You might think news reporting is **immediate**, but it isn't. It's **mediated**. Like all human communication, it has to be put into a material form – words, gestures, songs, pictures, writing. The point of mediating things is to communicate across space and time with as many people as possible. So the first thing to consider is that the media can reach **vast numbers of people**. Second, the messages nowadays are mediated by **highly advanced technology**.

Third, while there is the choice of making our own music or drawing our own cartoons, most of us opt to be **consumers** of the professional productions of relatively few corporations. These mega-companies are pretty much closed and centralized, but the reception is **public** and **dispersed**.

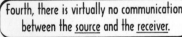

Fourth, there is virtually no communication between the <u>source</u> and the <u>receiver</u>.

Pop fiction falls between the
private and personal world of the home
and the outside world of the publishers, studios, record labels
and broadcasters, massive corporations which threaten to turn the
most fundamental quality of human beings - our unending love of
communication - into big business and, at its worst, propaganda.

On average, we spend over 15 years of our waking lives just watching television. Films, videos and the time spent reading newspapers and magazines, listening to music and surfing the Net, means that we spend **one-third** of our lives immersed in the media. Our abilities to speak, think, form relationships with others, even our dreams and our own sense of identity are now shaped by the media. So, studying the media is studying ourselves as social creatures.

9

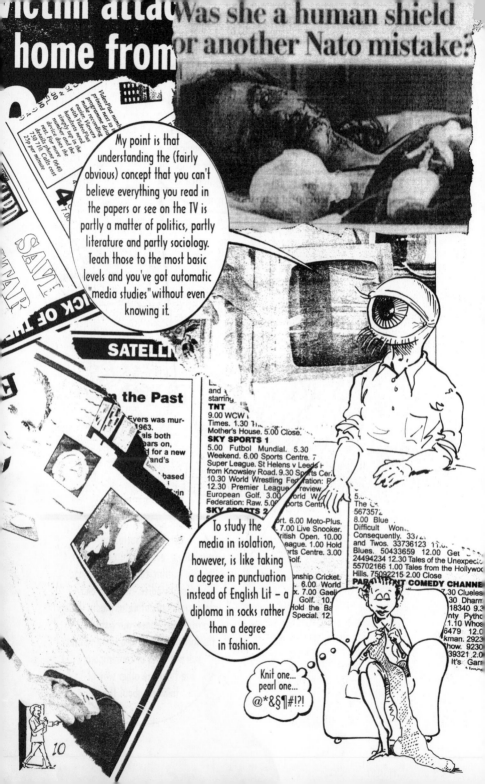

Was she a human shield or another Nato mistake?

My point is that understanding the (fairly obvious) concept that you can't believe everything you read in the papers or see on the TV is partly a matter of politics, partly literature and partly sociology. Teach those to the most basic levels and you've got automatic "media studies" without even knowing it.

SATELLI

the Past

...Evers was mur-...1963. ...als both ...ears on, ...d for a new ...and's

...based

To study the media in isolation, however, is like taking a degree in punctuation instead of English Lit – a diploma in socks rather than a degree in fashion.

TNT
9.00 WCW ...
Times. 1.30 T...
Mother's House. 5.00 Close.
SKY SPORTS 1
5.00 Futbol Mundial. 5.30
Weekend. 6.00 Sports Centre. 7...
Super League. St Helens v Leeds ...
from Knowsley Road. 9.30 Sports Cer...
10.30 World Wrestling Fed...ation: P...
12.30 Premier League ...review.
European Golf. 3.00 ...orld W...
Federation: Raw. 5.00 ...ports Centr...
SKY SPORTS 2
...ort. 6.00 Moto-Plus.
...7.00 Live Snooker.
...ritish Open. 10.00
...eague. 1.00 Hold
...rts Centre. 3.00
...olf.
...onship Cricket.
...x. 6.00 World
...x. 7.00 Gaeli...
...Golf. 10...
...Hold the Ba...
...Special. 12...

5....
The ...
567357...
8.00 Blue
Difficult Wo...
Consequently. 33/2...
and Twos. 33736123 11...
Blues. 50433659 12.00 Get
24494234 12.30 Tales of the Unexpec...
55702166 1.00 Tales from the Hollywo...
Hills. 75092215 2.00 Close
PAR...NT COMEDY CHANNE...
...30 Clueles...
...30 Dharm...
...18340 9.3...
...nty Pytho...
...1.10 Whos...
...6479 12.0...
...kman. 2923...
...how. 9230...
...39321 2.0...
...It's Garr...

Knit one...
pearl one...
@*&§¶#!?!

10

In today's globalized and interconnected world, it is foolish to imagine that anything can be studied in isolation.

The written word is only one medium in an audiovisual world. Changing the media changes everything: all politics, all literature, all society. Media studies is larger than these other disciplines. It tells us why politics, art and society are like they are, and how the future can be shaped for the best. These ideas can't just be conjured out of the haphazard opinions of metropolitan literati. They have to be studied systematically.

The advertising for Sunny Delight is a classic example of "pester power". It was linked to a healthy lifestyle for children and putting parents at ease. Since it contained vitamins A, B (1&6) and C, the parents thought it was healthier than conventional brands such as Coke and Pepsi. Sunny Delight also sponsored the English Basketball Association and blitzed schools with balls sporting the drink's logo.

Kids across Britain went glassy eyed with desire for Sunny D and pestered their parents for it in the supermarkets.

Mums complied and packed the drink into their children's lunch boxes.

But the Food Commission, an independent watchdog, has now declared Sunny Delight to be no better than conventional carbonated drinks. Its main ingredient is refined white sugar.

Food Commission Spokesperson:

Sunny Delight is full of thickeners, colours and flavourings to make it look like a fruit juice, when it is basically just a very sugary drink. It is just a marketing con.

Advertising has always been a form of propaganda. But now younger and younger children are being targeted. Deregulation has meant that there is no control on the amount of advertising that children are subjected to.

Many children's cartoons are little more than programme-length commercials. The first of these was the *He-Man* cartoon which promoted action figures and dolls of the same name.

Children are being sold everything from GI Joe to Teletubbies in the guise of TV shows.

Advertising for multinational products like McDonald's hamburgers, computer games and football T-shirts are specifically directed towards children. Hence the concern of Broadcasting Standards Commission.

BSC spokesperson:

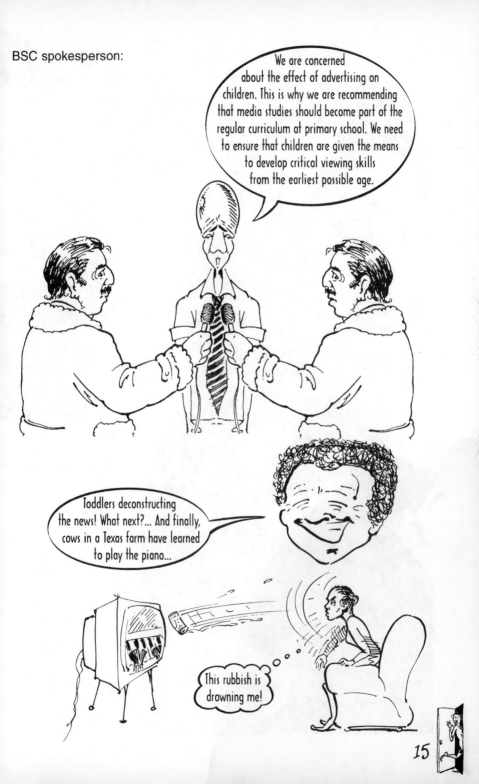

MEDIA AS INDUSTRY

Television, radio, films, videos, newspapers, magazines, comics are all cultural productions.

Cultural products are different from mundane products such as microwave ovens or vacuum cleaners. They contain meanings, values, ideas and are a form of communication. Moreover, they work on several levels.

A film like *The Seven Samurai* (1954) can be seen simply as a form of entertainment to be enjoyed, or as a work of art to be appreciated, or as a comment on feudal Japan.

It can also be seen as a classic with a universal message that can originate equally well from Hollywood in the form of <u>The Magnificent Seven</u>...(1960)

...or from India's own Bollywood in the shape of <u>Sholay.</u>(1975)

But like microwave ovens and vacuum cleaners, media products are mass-produced and marketed as consumer goods. Tabloid newspapers and lifestyle magazines sell in millions. TV programmes are watched by tens of millions. Films and videos are seen by hundreds of millions. And like industrial products, they require constant innovation and have to be sold as cheaply as possible.

Just as last year's "hot" model of car loses its shine, so there is a constant thirst for novelty in cultural production.

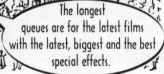

NEW MODEL £80,000

The longest queues are for the latest films with the latest, biggest and the best special effects.

Television

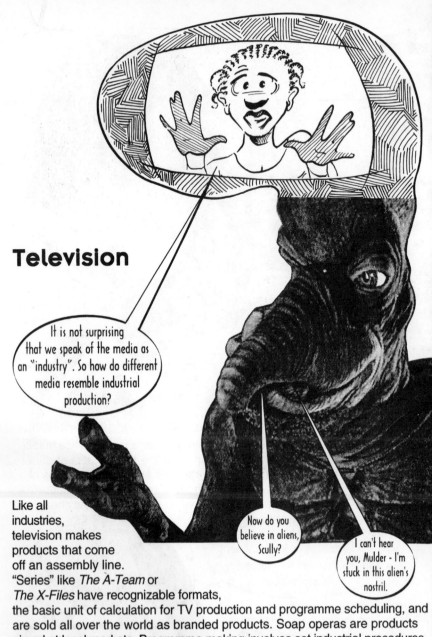

It is not surprising that we speak of the media as an "industry". So how do different media resemble industrial production?

Now do you believe in aliens, Scully?

I can't hear you, Mulder - I'm stuck in this alien's nostril.

Like all industries, television makes products that come off an assembly line. "Series" like *The A-Team* or *The X-Files* have recognizable formats, the basic unit of calculation for TV production and programme scheduling, and are sold all over the world as branded products. Soap operas are products aimed at local markets. Programme-making involves set industrial procedures. "Management" (controllers, managers, executive producers) and "workers" (producers, editors, researchers) are always at odds with each other. In most cases, ratings and advertising dictate what the viewers see on their TV screens.

Film

Studios act
as manufacturers
nursing their products
from conception to mass-
marketing. Hollywood was
most industrialized during the
1930s and 40s. Major companies
such as MGM and Warner Brothers
formed a monopoly – the Motion Picture
Producers and Distributors of America –
preventing any new competition.

They had support
from the banks and bought up
studios, networks and cinema chains,
thus controlling the availability of their
products. Later, major studios
went on to make similar
acquisitions abroad.

The structure of films became very stylized –
"problem" followed by "solution" – because this was
a commercial success. Variation became limited and audiences
were presented with easily recognizable products. Although "independents"
have more opportunity nowadays, big studios, such as Disney, still call
most of the shots.

Newspapers, Magazines and Alternative News

This is a fiercely competitive industry in which price-cutting, free offers, "takeovers" and mergers are not uncommon. The rise of alternative sources of news, from the Internet to 24-hour news channels (such as CNN, BBC News 24 and Sky News), has increased the competition. Niche marketing – the targeting of a specific group of consumers – has also appeared to encourage particular types of consumers and advertisers.

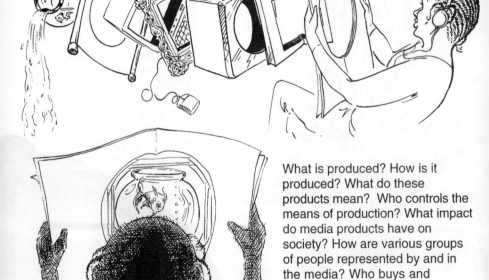

Media studies looks at the whole of the media industry from a number of different perspectives.

What is produced? How is it produced? What do these products mean? Who controls the means of production? What impact do media products have on society? How are various groups of people represented by and in the media? Who buys and consumes media products? How do the consumers interpret media products?

Attempts to answer these questions have been based on a number of different approaches which are reflected in the history and evolution of media studies.

The Evolution of Media Studies

The History Channel

Pre-film script for a documentary on the history of media studies.

OPENING SEQUENCE

MACMEDIA on an inner city street.
Lower Frame Super:
Walter MacMedia,
Star Presenter,
Globelink TV

<u>PRESENTER TO CAM</u>

The origins of media studies lie in American mass communication studies that emerged in the 1930s. There was widespread belief at the time that new urban areas were populated by a "mass" of faceless individuals who were rootless and deprived of certain social activities that previously existed, such as the presence of the family and strongly knit village communities. These people were therefore thought to be vulnerable to mass communication.

FACELESS INDIVIDUALS.
Nazi Camps

<u>VOICE OVER</u>

The case of Nazi Germany, where popular support for the Third Reich was won through the use of press, radio and propaganda films, strengthened this belief.

21

All history is His Story. Where is the women's viewpoint?

FREEZE FRAME on Columbia University.
S/I Subtitle: **The Functionalist Approach**

V/O

Mass communications studies peaked during the 1940s when the Bureau of Applied Social Research was established at Columbia University. The Bureau became one of the major centres of communications research in North America from the 1940s onwards.

Paul Lazarsfeld, one of the founders of the BASR, argued that media has administrative functions and enforces existing social forms. The functions of mass media were...

1. To confer status on public issues, organizations and social movements by selecting them for distribution within the public sphere. One issue among many is chosen for discussion and highlighting, and one or two representatives of the various lobby groups are selected for media participation.

2. Exposing deviants and their activities leads to an enforcement of what is regarded as normal. The status quo is maintained by the continuous portrayal of "criminals" or other forms of social deviants. This provides a conception of the Other against which the self of society can be maintained.

3. Reduce active public action. People are too busy consuming.

CAPTIONS

22

This functionalist school also viewed the mass media as offering a platform for the propaganda of social objectives. This was achieved in three ways.

1. **Monopolization –** don't give air space to others.
2. **Canalization** - don't give others a platform on the media.
3. **Supplementation –** back up the media message with face-to-face interaction.

CAPTIONS

These techniques apply equally to advertising.

V/O

In an influential study, *The People's Choice* (1944), Lazarsfeld and his colleagues attempted to discover the influence of the media over American voters.

People's PM...

...or is it the *Sun* wot did it?

PHOTO FINISH

Sun

If Kinnock wins today will the last person to leave Britain please turn out the lights

23

We used a panel sample over six months to study voters during a presidential campaign. We discovered that voting intentions were very resistant to media influence. A majority of our sample already had very well-defined political views: a predisposition which was increased by selective media exposure. People read the newspapers which supported their own views. When confronted with challenging ideas, voters simply filtered out messages that did not fit their preconceptions. Only 5% of our sample were actually converted.

LSF: P Lazarsfeld,
Columbia University

V/O

The period between the 1940s and the 1960s was dominated by "effects studies" of the mass media on the public.

FLOWER CHILDREN,
Woodstock.
Freeze frame on
Woodstock.
S/I Subtitle:
Effects Studies

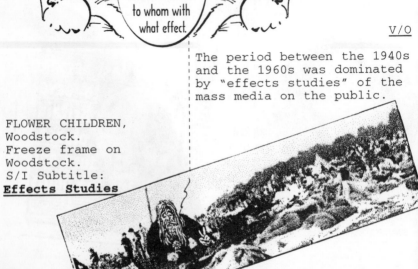

AUDIENCE -

The emphasis now shifted from the audience as unsuspecting anonymous mass to individuals who belonged to various social groups. Leaders within these groups would interpret information for its members. This process was known as the "two step flow" model. Individuals, the researchers argued, were not equal in face of media campaigns, but have different roles in the communication process — those who are active and pass on contacts and those that rely on other personal contacts. The public was as capable of rejecting certain messages as it was of accepting others.

What about black leaders?

V/O

Mass communication reinforced existing public opinion on four levels.
1. Predisposition and derived processes of selective exposure, selective perception and selective retention.
2. The norms of the group to which the member belongs.
3. Inter-personal dissemination of communication content.
4. The opinions of leaders and opinion-formers.

We will fight them on the beaches...

CAPTIONS.

25

LSF: J.T.Klapper

A number of researchers also argued that mass media lowered cultural standards through its excessively popular outputs.

We would all agree, I believe, that a great proportion of the material on the mass media is on a rather low aesthetic and intellectual level.

PUNDIT SYNC

V/O

Are there any black pundits in this thing?

There was also concern over the effect of screen violence and crime on children. But early work on violence found little support of effect on children. In Britain the first notable media research studied the impact of television on the behaviour of children. H. Himmelweit and his colleagues looked at 1,854 matched viewers and non-viewers in four British cities where TV was recently introduced. They found that television induced some anxieties about growing up in 13 to 14 years olds – and raised levels of job aspiration for the same group. But there was no important effect on desires and expectations of marriage. Television exerted influence only where views were put over repeatedly, preferably in dramatic form – and only if views were not already firmly fixed or the information given was not already obtained from other sources.

B/W CLIP of people watching b/w tv. Clip from *Child's play*. Children watching tv.

26

VIETNAM
demonstrations.

V/O

From the 1960s onwards, the media began to be viewed as ideology. This was largely a result of the social upheaval of the times. The anti-Vietnam war movement and the strikes of workers and students led to a more critical analysis. Effects studies were criticized for asking the wrong questions. Political effects were now seen as much more complex than the media's impact on voters.

V/O

THIS THING IS CALLED A "BOOK".

More specifically, it was argued that the "effects model"...

1. Tackled social problems backwards (it should start with perpetrators of violence, not with mass media).
2. Saw children as inadequate non-adults.
3. Was based on conservative assumptions.
4. Defined the subject of study inadequately.
5. Was based on studies with misapplied methodology (for example, it saw correlation as causality).
6. Was selective in its criticisms of media depictions of violence.
7. Saw the masses as inferior.
8. Made no attempt to understand meanings of media.
9. Was not grounded in theory.

CAPTIONS.

and onion

Questions were also raised about the long-term effects of the media. How were these long-term effects to be measured? These questions gave rise to **cultivation theory**.

MACMEDIA at
Lunatic asylum.

PRESENTER TO CAM

Cultivation theory, initiated by George Gerbner, began the "Cultural Indicators" research project in the mid-1960s within the "effects" tradition. Cultivation theorists argued that television has long-term effects which are small, gradual, indirect but cumulative and significant. They saw mass media as a socializing agent. Gerbner argued that the over-representation of violence on television constitutes a symbolic message about law and order, rather than being a simple cause of more aggressive behaviour by viewers. For instance, the action-adventure genre acts to reinforce a faith in law and order, the status quo and social justice (baddies usually get their just deserts).

FREEZE FRAME on
stylised violence.
S/I Subtitle:
Cultivation Theory.
More violence

Gerbner and his colleagues analysed sample weeks of prime-time and daytime television programming. In a survey of about 450 New Jersey schoolchildren, 73 per cent of heavy viewers compared to 62 per cent of light viewers gave 'TV' as the answer to a question asking them to describe what violence they had seen in a typical week. The difference in the pattern of responses between light and heavy viewers (when other variables are controlled), was labelled the 'cultivation differential' by Gerbner – it reflects the extent to which an attitude seems to be shaped by watching television. Misjudging the amount of violence in society is called the 'mean world syndrome'. Heavy viewers tend to believe that the world is a nastier place than do light viewers.

Gerbner has been criticized for over-simplification.

PEOPLE watching violence on TV.

LFS: Denis McQuail, author of *Mass Communication Theory* (1987)

PUNDIT SYNC

It is almost impossible to deal convincingly with the complexity of posited relationships between symbolic structures, audience behaviour and audience views, given the many intervening and powerful social background factors.

The passive audience of the 1960s became the active audience of the 1970s in the **Uses and Gratifications Theory** of Elihu Katz and others. This reversed the imbalance of earlier theories, in that it advocated a more active role for the viewer. According to this theory, the viewer views the media as a utility in a self-confirmatory manner (this corresponded with the social psychological theory of social cognition). Certain items are selected from the media, either because they provide gratification for entertainment, or for utility needs. According to Katz, the gratification approach emphasizes...

SEX SEQUENCE from a film. Freeze frame on gratified man.
S/I Subtitle:
Uses and Gratifications

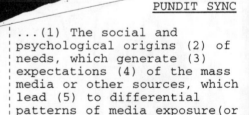

Will this do, Brian?

PUNDIT SYNC

...(1) The social and psychological origins (2) of needs, which generate (3) expectations (4) of the mass media or other sources, which lead (5) to differential patterns of media exposure(or engagement in other activities), resulting (6) in need gratifications and (7) other consequences, perhaps mostly unintended ones.

LFS: E. Katz

Denis McQuail suggests that
the media serves four main
types of needs...
Diversion – emotional release
to avoid problems or work.
Personal relationship –
provides company when alone
and becomes a subject of
discussion with others.
Personal identity – assesses
and locates our own selves
against the social world.
Surveillance – provides
information about issues and
events.

CAPTION

PUNDIT SYNC

"Media use is most suitably
characterized as an
interactive process, relating
media content, individual
needs, perceptions, roles and
values and the social context
in which a person is
situated."

LFS: McQuail

Other researchers made a
distinction between
gratification sought and
gratification obtained.

PUNDIT SYNC

...to concentrate less on
what the media do to people
than on what people do with
the media.

LFS: McQuail

V/O

The gratification approach
was criticized for being
individualistic, empiricist,
mentalistic. That is, it was
too functionalist and did not
include society and welfare.
It was also cyclic and
tautological: consumption
leads to gratification of
need and need leads to
satisfaction through
functional behaviour.

PEOPLE consuming

V/O

The Marxist approach to media studies developed in parallel with the functionalist approach. It is best characterized by the work of the **Frankfurt School**.

STILL PHOTO of Marx.
S/I Subtitle:
Marxist Approach

V/O

The Frankfurt School consists of a group of loosely connected intellectuals who took their name from the **Institute for Social Research** founded in Frankfurt, Germany, in 1923. The school was concerned with developing a revolutionary, philosophical variant of Western Marxism, opposed to capitalism in the West and Stalinism in the East, which came to be called **critical theory**. During the 1930s, when Hitler came to power, the Institute was forced to leave Germany for New York. In 1953, it was re-established in Frankfurt. Members of the School included T.W. Adorno, Max Horkheimer, Herbert Marcuse, Eric Fromm and Walter Benjamin. Jürgen Habermas continues the tradition of the Frankfurt School.

Establisher of Frankfurt. Stills of Theodor Adorno, Max Horkheimer, Herbert Marcuse, Eric Fromm, Walter Benjamin and Jürgen Habermas.
Caption on still of Adorno: **The Frankfurt School**

SHOULDN'T THERE BE SIX OF US?

ESTABLISHER of New York. People queuing outside cinema.

Adorno and Horkheimer developed a Marxist sociological approach to media studies at the New York-based Institute for Social Research. They saw the media as a **cultural industry** that maintained power relations and served to lessen the "resistance standards" of cultural aesthetics by popularizing certain types of culture. The values perpetuated by the media were contradictory to the values of the radical Enlightenment tradition. The masses are "dumbed" by the banality of the media. Their ability to function efficiently as citizens in a democratic state is replaced by their ceaseless consumption of culture or products, or both.

Though the functionalist and Marxist approaches are radically different in their underlying assumptions, they are similar in that they both presume audiences to be passive and powerless.

According to Adorno, the listener to industrialized and commodified popular music is caught up in a standardized and routinized set of responses. In particular, Adorno argues that he or she is distracted and inattentive. In this sense, pop music is part of the everyday background of contemporary social life. For example, we do not listen to it in the way that musical experts think that we should listen to a Beethoven symphony, that is, by sitting down and giving it all our attention, and seeing how the parts relate to the whole in creating the kind of meaning that Beethoven intended to communicate. In Adorno's view, the pleasure derived from pop music is superficial and false. Thus the listener may be what Adorno calls 'rhythmically obedient'. He or she is 'slave to the rhythm', following the standardized beat of the song and becoming overpowered by it. For Adorno, individuals who enjoy these pleasures are corrupted by immersion and are open to the domination of the industrialized, capitalist system.

SLAVE TO

THE RHYTHM

TOKEN BLACK PRESENCE

LFS: Nicholas Abercrombie, Professor of Sociology, University of Lancaster

This sync is too bloody long. Don't they know at the History Channel that syncs longer than 40 seconds are just too boring.

This argument was not accepted by everyone. In the early 1960s, for example, Canadian literary scholar **Marshall McLuhan** (1911–80) argued that the content of the media was largely irrelevant. What was important was the way each new medium disrupted tradition and reshaped the social and cultural environment. McLuhan's argument was summed up in his famous soundbite:

CAPTION on still
'the medium is the message'

The content of the message is only like a juicy piece of meat that a burglar uses to distract the watchdogs of the mind. It is the *medium* that shapes the mind. During my study of the invention of the printing press, I noticed that the shift from the oral to the print medium actually changed the senses and perceptions of 15th-century society. Print intensified the visual and separated it from other senses, particularly sound.

Indeed, print media was instrumental in creating a sensory environment that produced Western capitalist societies - an environment that was bureaucratic and organized around mass production, an ideology of individualism, and commitment to the Nation State as the fundamental social unit.

LFS: Marshall McLuhan, author, *The Gutenberg Galaxy* (1962)

V/O

McLuhan went on to study the shift from print to the electronic medium. He argued that television was reconnecting the senses that were fragmented by print. Electronic media was taking society back to a kind of pre-print state of harmony. He predicted the emergence of a new 'global village' in which communication technologies would bring the people of the planet closer together.

McLuhan's theories were a sophisticated version of technological determinism. He saw each medium as shaping our senses to produce certain inevitable social outcomes. Moreover, the all-pervasive nature of the medium made it virtually impossible for ordinary people to notice how technology was really influencing them.

Satellite and television's shrinking the globe!

Media studies changed direction again in the mid-1960s with **semiology** and the concept of 'text'. **Roland Barthes** (1915-80) showed that any kind of popular culture could be decoded by means of reading the 'signs' within the text. Now, the problem was: did the meanings reside within the text, or was the audience the source of meaning? This debate continued into the 1970s and 80s as media studies became firmly grounded in the notion of an active audience as opposed to the passive audience of earlier Marxist or functionalist theories. This is in part due to the influence of semiological, structuralist and post-structuralist thinkers such as **Ferdinand de Saussure** (1857-1913), **Michel Foucault** (1926-84) and **Jacques Derrida** (b. 1930) who, through their deconstruction of the text and ideology of empowerment against dominant discourses, provide the viewer with the possibility of a more active role.

Closing credits.
Roller.
Overall RT:0.50″

Who the heck is Saussure?

SUNDAY ^{THE} THEORY

"THE PEOPLE'S VOICE"   25th August, 1915

LINGUIST DISCOVERS MEANING

Janet Street Smart *reports on the discovery of the science of signs in the Swiss Alps*

An Alp yesterday

A Swiss linguist is claiming a breakthrough in the understanding of meaning.

Ferdinand de Saussure, Professor of General Linguistics, University of Geneva, says that meaning can be found everywhere. All the social and cultural phenomena that surround us are not just material objects or events. They are objects and events which contain signs. Moreover, the objects and events are defined by a network of relations. We can decode meaning if we learn to read signs and appreciate relations.

(continued page 2)

SAUCY SAUSSURE & THE MEANING OF LIFE

(from page 1)

"I am suggesting that we should treat all phenomena as though they were languages," says Professor Saussure. "Just as languages have words which are brought together to form meaningful sentences by syntax and grammar, so material phenomena contain signs that are given meaning by a system of relations," he adds. Elaborating the analogy, he describes all sign systems as "texts"

In a shortly to be published book, *Course in General Linguistics* (published in 1916), Professor Saussure divides the sign into two components: the signifier, or "sound image", and the signified, or "concept". He also suggests that the relationship between the signifiers and the signified is arbitrary.

There is no logical connection between a word and a concept or a signifier and signified.

We should treat social and cultural phenomena as texts and not as things per se. This will emphasize that relationships are all-important.

Thus, the word "tree" and the concept tree have no sensible connection.

A tree

FOR-EIGN NEWS

War: progress slow on Eastern front FULL REPORT PAGE 22-3

40

"IT'S A TIME OF THE SIGNS" CLAIMS TOP BOFFIN

Professor Saussure calls his science of signs, or "a science that studies the life of signs at the heart of social life" as he puts it, semiology.

Reactions to Professor Saussure's discovery have been divided. Roland Barthes at the Ecole Pratique des Hautes Etudes in Paris, describes it as a "breakthrough in the sociology of signs, symbols and representations".

Ted Crilly, Bishop of Craggy Island, says semiology is a new religious cult.

Feck! The esoteric language of semiologists is not too far removed from that of Gnostic and pagan groups.

It will challenge our traditional assumptions of the status of the author, treatment of language, interpretations of text and the idea of history.

Signs and Symbols, p.43
Leader, Section 2, p.42
Weather p.46, Bingo p.90
Cryptic Crossword p.119

This is damn sight harder than editing a bus ticket!

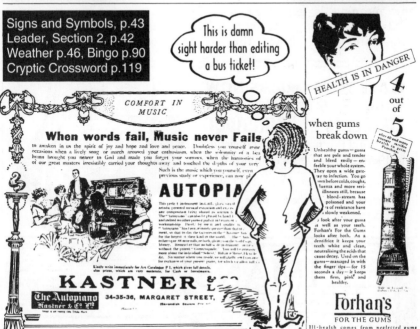

41

The SUNDAY THEORY

1 Fleet Street, London WC1. Telephone: 231 5679. Cable: theory.com

Patience, not panic, key to understanding semiology

The first reaction is one of weary astonishment. Another new discovery hailed as the panacea for all our ills. As reported in our front-page today, the new science of Semiology is said to unearth meaning from all variety of social and cultural products.

On first sight, this looks like a large claim. But as far as we can ascertain, Professor Saussure is a highly respected linguist, although his work is based on controversial new principles.

Semiology is concerned with how meaning is generated in "texts". It deals with what signs are and how they function. It is a new language that may enable us to look at films, television shows, fashion, food, works of art, and much else besides in a new way. We may thus be better equipped to deal with codes, formulas, genres, the "language" of television, and the grammar of cinema.

We would urge critics of Professor Saussure, like Bishop Crilly, to be patient. Meaning is a thorny territory, much fought over by all sections of society. But surely something that explores how meaning is generated and conveyed deserves serious attention from all of us.

If you can see it or hear it, you can read it

Can't tell your symbol from your sign? Your metaphor from metonymy? Confused? Well, you needn't be, with our guide to key concepts in media theory.

By **Charlotte Brighteyes**

Sign: an inseparable combination of a concept and a sound-image. A Sign must have physical forms, must refer to something other than itself and be recognized as a sign by people.

Flowers have physical form, but when presented to a person they become a sign, most commonly, of love.

A sign is divided into two components: the **signifier** which is its physical form perceived by our physical senses; and the **signified** which is the mental concept to which the sign refers.

Symbol: unlike a sign, a symbol does not have an arbitrary signifier. Saussure says:

One characteristic of the symbol is that it is never wholly arbitrary; it is not empty, for there is a rudiment of a natural bond between the signifier and signified.

The symbol of justice, a pair of scales, could not be replaced by just another symbol, such as a chariot.

Code: a system of signs based on culturally agreed rules. Codes allow specific cultures to communicate through the use of signs.

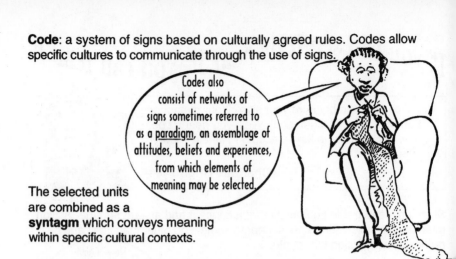

Codes also consist of networks of signs sometimes referred to as a <u>paradigm</u>, an assemblage of attitudes, beliefs and experiences, from which elements of meaning may be selected.

The selected units are combined as a **syntagm** which conveys meaning within specific cultural contexts.

Text: a signifying structure composed of signs and codes.

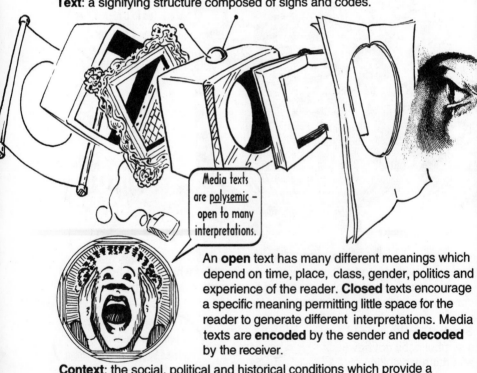

Media texts are <u>polysemic</u> – open to many interpretations.

An **open** text has many different meanings which depend on time, place, class, gender, politics and experience of the reader. **Closed** texts encourage a specific meaning permitting little space for the reader to generate different interpretations. Media texts are **encoded** by the sender and **decoded** by the receiver.

Context: the social, political and historical conditions which provide a structure and within which certain actions, processes or events are located and have meaning.

Reading: the process of interaction when a text is analysed as well as the final result of that process, the interpretation.

44

Intertextuality: the reading of a text in the light of others of similar nature. Intertextuality can create extra layers of meaning and associations leading to an understanding of a text that is based partly on what precedes it, or may follow it, or other media texts in other contexts. Intertextuality is often produced deliberately to create references which an audience can easily recognize. A well-known example is the advertisement of Carling Black Label lager which was set in a laundry and mimicked another advertisement for Levi Jeans that itself included a 1960s soul record and iconic 1950s James Dean images.

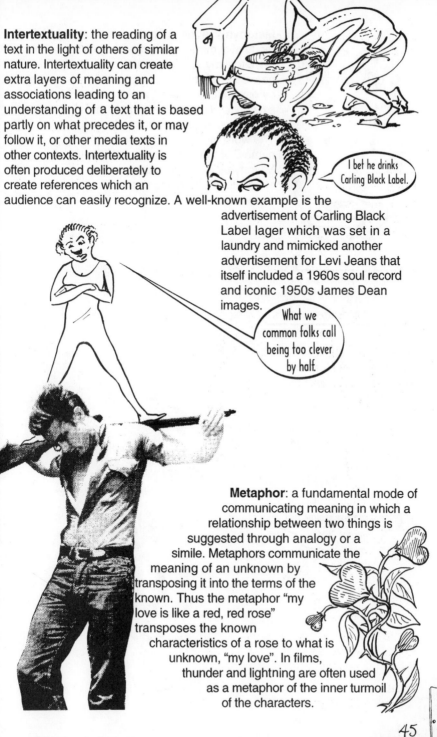

I bet he drinks Carling Black Label.

What we common folks call being too clever by half.

Metaphor: a fundamental mode of communicating meaning in which a relationship between two things is suggested through analogy or a simile. Metaphors communicate the meaning of an unknown by transposing it into the terms of the known. Thus the metaphor "my love is like a red, red rose" transposes the known characteristics of a rose to what is unknown, "my love". In films, thunder and lightning are often used as a metaphor of the inner turmoil of the characters.

45

Metonymy: another fundamental mode of communicating meaning. In metonymy, a relationship between two things is suggested by association, implying the existence of codes that enable the proper connections to be made. The word means "transposed names" or "substitute meaning". Metonymy works by using parts or elements of something to stand for the whole.

For example, we often use the term "the crown" to speak of the Queen or the idea of monarchy as a whole.

News is metonymic: a reported event is often interpreted to represent the whole of reality.

An example of metonymy is the monstrous balloon, Rover, in the cult television series The Prisoner,* standing for the oppressive regime that runs the Village.

*first shown 1967/68

Narrative: the process as well as the end product of story-telling and

mental activity that organizes data into patterns or cause-and-effect chains of events. Narrative is an important feature of print and broadcast journalism

where codes determine the structure, order and components of a story. The basic narrative structure of a news story is the same as that of a situation comedy or a detective show: in both cases, "a state of equilibrium is

disrupted, the forces of disruption are worked through until a resolution is reached, and another state of equilibrium is achieved." We make sense of our lives by rendering our lives as narratives. Biography, the narratives of

other peoples' lives, is an important way of giving meaning to our own lives.

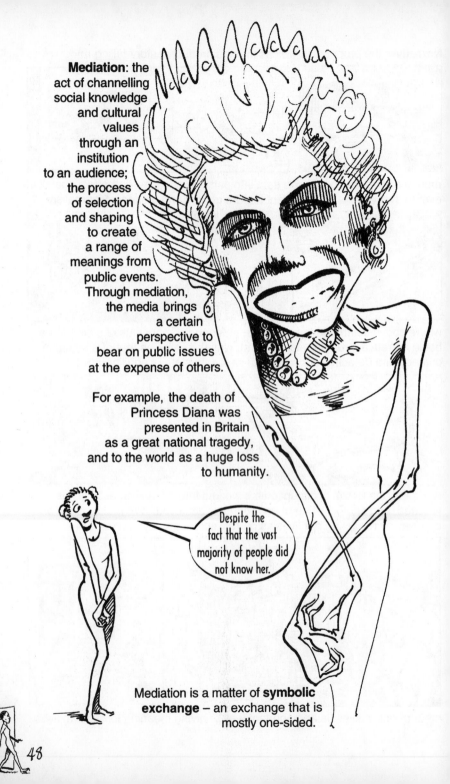

Mediation: the act of channelling social knowledge and cultural values through an institution to an audience; the process of selection and shaping to create a range of meanings from public events. Through mediation, the media brings a certain perspective to bear on public issues at the expense of others.

For example, the death of Princess Diana was presented in Britain as a great national tragedy, and to the world as a huge loss to humanity.

Despite the fact that the vast majority of people did not know her.

Mediation is a matter of **symbolic exchange** – an exchange that is mostly one-sided.

Genre: the categories of media products; specific types of books, film, television and radio programmes. Genres are identified by their conventions which the audience recognize through regular contact. The term originated in literary criticism but was adoted by cinema studies. Television is exclusively genre-led.

Discourse: structured representation of events; structured and inter-related interpretation of social and cultural knowledge that express power relations. The term suggests that the very act of referring to, or interpreting, the world is also **making** the world.

Varieties ‖ Media Studies

During the 1980s, the theoretical background to media studies changed significantly. Research on the media became more thoroughly grounded on empirical work. A number of new approaches to studying the media appeared – these are now the main varieties of media studies.

Institutional Studies

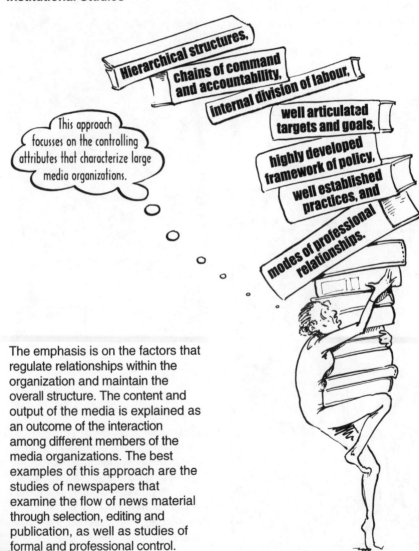

This approach focusses on the controlling attributes that characterize large media organizations.

Hierarchical structures, chains of command and accountability, internal division of labour, well articulated targets and goals, highly developed framework of policy, well established practices, and modes of professional relationships.

The emphasis is on the factors that regulate relationships within the organization and maintain the overall structure. The content and output of the media is explained as an outcome of the interaction among different members of the media organizations. The best examples of this approach are the studies of newspapers that examine the flow of news material through selection, editing and publication, as well as studies of formal and professional control.

Professional Ideologies

Media professionals claim to be objective and impartial. On the basis of this claim, journalists and broadcasters seek autonomy within their industry. Professional standards and ethics further enable journalists to resist "outside" pressures from the public or lobbyist groups and "internal" control from owners, management and government. Studies of beliefs, values and practices look at the attributes of professionalism within the media.

What are the constraints on the autonomy of media professionals?

How is influence exercised?

What compromises does the internal culture of cooperation produce?

The Politics of Integrity

Professional integrity is compromised by a number of factors. Owners of newspapers and magazines may veto the decisions of editors. The editors often override the opinion of the reporters. Newspapers generally follow a political line and promote particular political ideologies – so they may alter or ignore stories that undermine their political position.

Most countries have laws that constrain the media. These are the most common:

§ The National Security Act or the Official Secrets Act that prevent the publication of certain information which is seen as prejudicial to the "national interest".

§ Laws that "protect" the public from indecent, corrupting or offensive material, such as the British Obscene Publications Act.

§ Libel laws that protect the individual from being unjustly accused or represented.

§ Blasphemy laws that protect religious beliefs and sentiments.

Negotiated Autonomy

All this means that media professionals are under constant pressure, their alleged independence under perpetual threat, and professional standards are always on the verge of being compromised. However, studies of professionalism in the media have identified a strong claim for professional autonomy. Jeremy Tunstall's ground-breaking studies of *Journalists at Work* have shown that journalists emphasize "non-revenue goals" and are apt at maintaining their autonomy by negotiating, insisting on not revealing their sources, and other means. The most famous example is that of the Watergate journalists, Bernstein and Woodward.

Structural Studies of the Media

Structural accounts of the media are based on semiotics and deconstruction –
a mode of philosophical analysis associated with the writings of French
philosopher Jacques Derrida. The fundamental concern here is with the
systems and processes of signification and representation.

The key to
this is the deconstruction
of such texts as advertisements,
photographs, television shows
and films.

Structuralist
media studies
are also informed by
the French Marxist philosopher **Louis
Althusser**'s (1918–90) reformulation of ideology as a representation of the
imaginary relationship of individuals with the real conditions of their existence.

Beyond Structuralism

In the 1970s, the combination of Althusserian Marxism and semiotics provided the main impetus for sustained work on media texts. But structuralist studies have now moved beyond Althusser. Poststructuralism, often hard to distinguish from structuralism, is more concerned with psychoanalytical theories and the role of pleasure in producing and regulating meanings.

So, poststructuralist studies of the media now attempt to combine the analysis of media-signifying practices with psychoanalysis.

Thus the relationship of texts to subjects is theorized. The subject here is not the unified subject of Althusser or of traditional Marxism, but a contradictory, de-centred subject displaced across a range of discourses in which he or she participates.

Political Economy

An alternative approach looks at the "political economy" of the media.
Political economy sees the relationship between ownership and political
power as the main area of influence in shaping media structures and output.

Examples of Political Economy

Commercial media institutions, such as NBC in the US, ITV in Britain, and ABC in Australia, are driven by advertising and the need to produce programmes that attract high ratings.

Media institutions that are controlled by the State, such as RTM in Malaysia, or whose revenues are acquired from the public purse, like the BBC, tend to cover the middle ground or move towards the dominant consensus.

Culturalist Studies of the Media

Culturalist studies of the media take an ambiguous position between the theoretical concerns of structuralism and political economy. Undertaken within the tradition of cultural studies, the emphasis here is on different frameworks of knowledge that encode and decode a programme. The difference is characterized by a symmetry of power distribution leading to three different types of readings.

Dominant - where the central meaning of the text is emphasized.

Negotiated - where there are slight disagreements but generally the main meaning of the text is accepted.

Oppositional - where the text is read in a contrary manner to its intended meaning - that is, according to how it has been encoded.

This theoretical framework is linked to the idea of *hegemony* first presented by the Italian activist and Marxist philosopher, **Antonio Gramsci** (1891-1937).

This view of media power was presented by **Stuart Hall** (b.1932) and his Cultural Studies colleagues in *Policing the Crisis* (1978).

This study applies the theory of hegemony and a sociology of "moral panic" to an account of the social production of news in post-war Britain.

Policing the Crisis argues that the economic and social crisis of the 1970s threatened the hegemony (the governing "consensus") of the British ruling classes. A series of social issues such as muggings, union unrest and student demonstrations were presented by the media as "moral panics". Different problems were presented by the media as a single monolithic crisis of law and order which demanded a firm hand.

This perceived breakdown in "law and order" paved the way for stronger state control to which the people gave willing consent.

The media's strongest weapon in maintaining the hegemony of the ruling classes was the access to primary definers of the crisis – "legitimate spokespeople" such as the police, the courts and politicians.

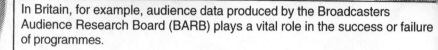

In Britain, for example, audience data produced by the Broadcasters Audience Research Board (BARB) plays a vital role in the success or failure of programmes.

The size of the audience that the media can now reach around the world has increased tremendously. Over two billion people may watch the football World Cup.

> But apart from <u>mass</u> audience, there are also <u>specific</u> audiences targeted for particular media products.

There is an audience for *NBC Nightly News*, as well as for the *MacNeil-Lehre NewsHour* which, like *Channel 4 News* in Britain, offers more in-depth analysis. There are audiences for the *National Enquirer*, which has no notion of news, for the British tabloid *The Sun*, in which there is not much distinction between news and (bigoted) opinion, and for *The Independent*, which takes news ever so seriously.

Specifying audiences

Specific audiences can be defined in three general ways:

- By particular products such as magazines, newspapers, films.
- By specific types of product such as women's magazines, particular genre of film, specific type of music – for example, the classical music audience.
- By their association to a particular social or geographical group according to age, gender, class, nation, ethnicity, religion, educational level, political allegiance, region, urban or rural background.

Media organizations carry out research to identify the size and nature of their respective audience. In the US, for example, the Nielsen ratings from the market research company, Nielsen Media Research, produce indicators of the relative popularity of television shows. The ratings are compiled by installing "people meters" in 4,000 selected homes. The meters record what is being watched in the house. Every two years, the "Nielsen households" are replaced to prevent biased or inaccurate measurements.

But how valid are such ratings? Do statistics gathered by media organizations really reflect audience perception of what they watch? The Nielsen ratings have been criticized for reflecting the habits of people who are hooked on television – the occasional or critical viewers who seek out particular programmes are excluded.

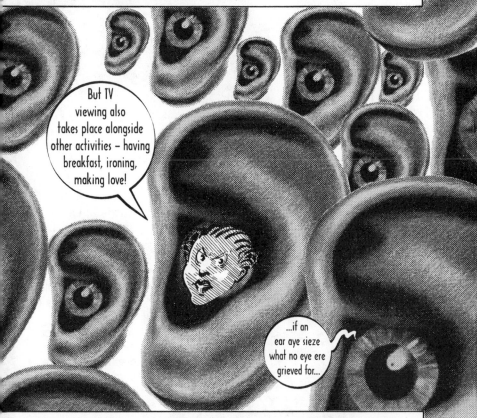

But TV viewing also takes place alongside other activities – having breakfast, ironing, making love!

...if an ear aye sieze what no eye ere grieved for...

Radio has been reduced to a tertiary mode of activity. It may be "on" but most people do not listen to it actively; it largely provides background music and "chat". Only inside the dark enclosure of the cinema, do audiences give their undivided attention to what they are consuming.

Dallas

An Audience Study

The 1980s American soap opera *Dallas*, the long-running saga of a Texan oil-made-rich family, has been the subject of numerous studies by media researchers. A famous study on cross-cultural interpretation of *Dallas* was conducted in 1993 by Elihu Katz, who was then at the Hebrew University of Jerusalem, and Tamar Liebes, Associate Professor in Communications, also at the Hebrew University.

Y'all go 'n' gitch'rself somethin' real pretty now – y'hear?

Katz and Liebes assembled focus groups each consisting of three married couples. The groups would view an episode of *Dallas*, and this would be followed by a guided discussion on the show. The participants would also be asked to complete a questionnaire on their normal viewing habits concerning *Dallas*.

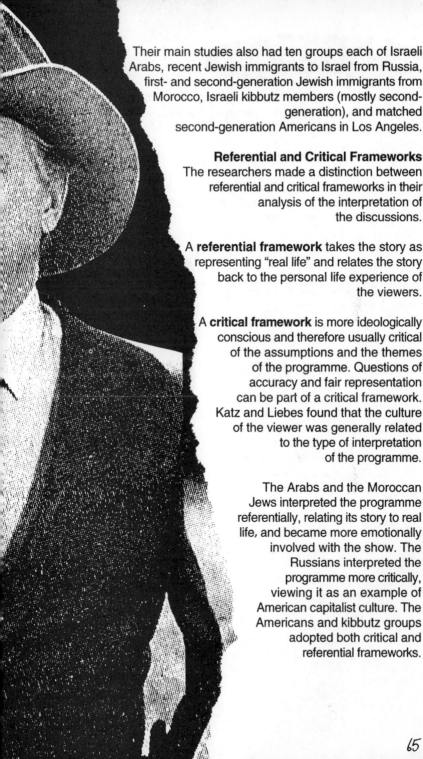

Their main studies also had ten groups each of Israeli Arabs, recent Jewish immigrants to Israel from Russia, first- and second-generation Jewish immigrants from Morocco, Israeli kibbutz members (mostly second-generation), and matched second-generation Americans in Los Angeles.

Referential and Critical Frameworks

The researchers made a distinction between referential and critical frameworks in their analysis of the interpretation of the discussions.

A **referential framework** takes the story as representing "real life" and relates the story back to the personal life experience of the viewers.

A **critical framework** is more ideologically conscious and therefore usually critical of the assumptions and the themes of the programme. Questions of accuracy and fair representation can be part of a critical framework. Katz and Liebes found that the culture of the viewer was generally related to the type of interpretation of the programme.

The Arabs and the Moroccan Jews interpreted the programme referentially, relating its story to real life, and became more emotionally involved with the show. The Russians interpreted the programme more critically, viewing it as an example of American capitalist culture. The Americans and kibbutz groups adopted both critical and referential frameworks.

forms of retelling

The researchers found that there were three different levels of analysis or "selective perception" across cultures.

Linear which focusses on the storyline.

Segmented which focusses on the personal and inter-personal development of characters in relation to feelings, problems and relationships.

Thematic which focusses on the message underlying the storyline.

The more traditional groups, such as the Arabs and Moroccans, tended to be linear and generally focussed on one of the storylines, usually following the trajectory of the hero trying to achieve his aims.

The Russian retellings tended to be thematic, suppressing the detail and involving political analysis. This led to statements about themes, ideology and the message of the show. There was a concern for the ideological motives of the producers – presumed as protagonists of the capitalist. The thematic level of analysis is closed and deterministic like linear interpretations, but has an ideological "determining force".

The kibbutz and American viewers interpreted the show through a segmented level of analysis, often focussing on relationships which were of psychological interests to the viewers themselves. These retellings tended to be open-ended and involved psychoanalytic perspectives.

As comparatively secure people, the kibbutz and American participants could "afford the luxury of interest in the individual (i.e. in themselves)".

POIT!

So, a particular media product can have different meanings for different social groups. To understand the potential meanings of media output, we need cultural maps of audiences that show the repertoire of cultural and symbolic resources available to different subgroups within specific groups of audiences.

In his famous studies on *Nationwide* in 1980, David Morley, Professor of Sociology at Goldsmiths College, University of London, tried to produce one such map.

NATIONWIDE: another Audience Study

During the 1970s, *Nationwide* had a regular early evening slot on BBC1, following the main national news from London. This current affairs programme included human-interest stories from "the regions", as well as a "down-to-earth" look at the major events of the day.

Morley examined how specific subgroups of the *Nationwide* audience read the programme.

He showed two programmes to 29 small groups of 2 to 13 people from different social, cultural and educational backgrounds. He discovered that different subgroups had sharply different readings of the programme.

<u>Dominant Readings</u> were common among:
·Print Management Trainees
·Bank Managers
·Apprentices
·School Students

<u>Negotiated Readings</u> were common among:
·Teacher-Training College Students
·University Arts Students
·Photography Higher Education Students
·Trade Union Officials

<u>Oppositional Readings</u> were common among:
· Black Further Education Students
· Trade Unionists active in the work-place

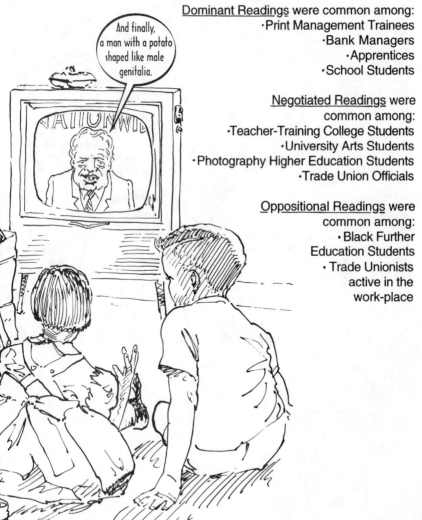

Situating the Audience

Whether a programme succeeded in transmitting the dominant meaning depended on whether its readers inhabited codes and ideologies acquired from established institutions like churches or schools or from institutions such as trade unions, or marginalized subcultures.

> People from the <u>same class</u> may read programmes differently, depending on the <u>institutions</u> in which they are situated.

> I conclude that competence in parliamentary democracy and economics is necessary for reading current affairs TV.

> The most competent people tended to be white, middle class and constructed through the discourses of masculinity.

> Wow, that really surprises me...

Representation

Through words, sounds and pictures, the various media produce a likeness of the "real" world. Through a process of mediation, they *re*-present the world to an audience. This *re*-presentation of reality is apparently similar to the way in which we interpret the world and create meaning for ourselves through our own physical senses. By constructing a representation of reality, the media constructs meanings about the world.

"Representation" has dual meanings: to "show" or present, and to "describe" or declare.

The term refers to the <u>process</u> as well as the <u>products</u> of making signs stand for their meanings.

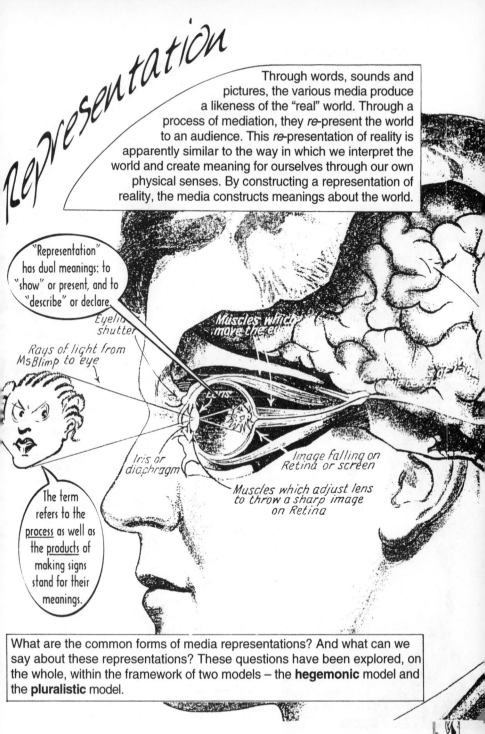

Eyelid shutter

Muscles which move the eye

Rays of light from MsBlimp to eye

Lens

Iris or diaphragm

Image falling on Retina or screen

Muscles which adjust lens to throw a sharp image on Retina

What are the common forms of media representations? And what can we say about these representations? These questions have been explored, on the whole, within the framework of two models – the **hegemonic** model and the **pluralistic** model.

The Hegemonic Model

The basic assumption of the hegemonic model is that the ruling classes are able to rule by ideas and cultural influence rather than force. Hegemony is the ability of the ruling classes to rule by consent, by evolving a consensus for the ruling sentiments through everyday cultural life, including media representation of the world.

message sent to association centre of brain

Earlier, "cruder" Marxist theories emphasized powerful groups distorting social reality and argued that the media was merely a mouthpiece of the ruling class.

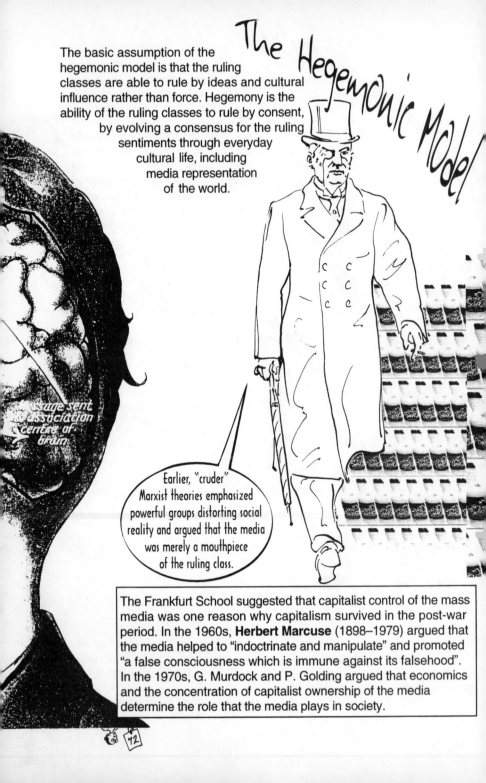

The Frankfurt School suggested that capitalist control of the mass media was one reason why capitalism survived in the post-war period. In the 1960s, **Herbert Marcuse** (1898–1979) argued that the media helped to "indoctrinate and manipulate" and promoted "a false consciousness which is immune against its falsehood". In the 1970s, G. Murdock and P. Golding argued that economics and the concentration of capitalist ownership of the media determine the role that the media plays in society.

More sophisticated hegemonic interpretations involve a combination of Althusser's reformulation of **ideology** and Roland Barthes' notion of **myth**. Althusser used the term "ideological state apparatus" to describe social institutions, such as the media, which represent capitalism as normal and inevitable. The media produce a "commonsense" which is really ideology.

Ideologies work through symbolic codes which explain and represent social, cultural and political reality.

I, Barthes, classified this symbolic representation as mythic.

Mythic representation is not simply false, but what appears to us as **natural**. Mythic symbols are important in shaping a culture's self-identity; they represent what are seen as eternal and immutable "truths". Because mythic representation is seen as self-evident and commonsensical, it is not often questioned.

The Pluralistic Model

The pluralistic model instead sees the media as diverse and full of consumer choices. The media, it is suggested, reflects the plurality of society, which consists of a number of competing interests and different viewpoints. The views and values that predominate in the media simply echo the consensus of the society. The main function of the media is to please the audience. It therefore seeks to fulfil their needs, and its representations meet with their expectations.

Moreover, as media "texts" are complex and contain multiple meanings, it is difficult to find clear patterns of representation or the distinct exercise of ideological power. Indeed, media representations themselves are pluralistic.

In Britain, certain media endorse the Queen and reflect the popular support of the monarchy.

But certain newspapers and satirical television shows ridicule and parody the Royal family.

The tendency of the media to recycle and parody other media items, makes the system of reading signs more complex and renders "ideological bias" meaningless.

Every representation is always already a _misrepresentation_. Both have grains of truth and are useful tools of analysis.

Stereotypes

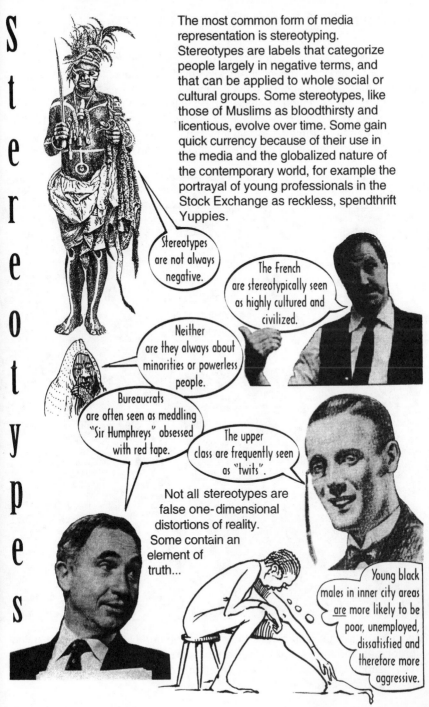

The most common form of media representation is stereotyping. Stereotypes are labels that categorize people largely in negative terms, and that can be applied to whole social or cultural groups. Some stereotypes, like those of Muslims as bloodthirsty and licentious, evolve over time. Some gain quick currency because of their use in the media and the globalized nature of the contemporary world, for example the portrayal of young professionals in the Stock Exchange as reckless, spendthrift Yuppies.

Stereotypes are not always negative.

The French are stereotypically seen as highly cultured and civilized.

Neither are they always about minorities or powerless people.

Bureaucrats are often seen as meddling "Sir Humphreys" obsessed with red tape.

The upper class are frequently seen as "twits".

Not all stereotypes are false one-dimensional distortions of reality. Some contain an element of truth...

Young black males in inner city areas _are_ more likely to be poor, unemployed, dissatisfied and therefore more aggressive.

Marginalizing the Stereotype

Ideologically, stereotypes are used to justify one's privileged position and differential treatment of others. If Africans could be represented as ignorant savages, then their treatment under colonialism could be justified and the contemporary exploitation of Africa can be validated. If rural people can be represented as useless peasants, their marginalization from the nation's economy can be excused. If dissidents can be classified as "perverts" and "deviants", then their harsh legal treatment can be argued as justly deserved.

Media texts contain stereotypes because of the need for economy. By using stereotypes, the media establishes an instant rapport with the audience. Thirty-second advertisements need shorthand characters in order to quickly gain audience recognition.

"Moral Panics"

Among the earliest studies of representation is Stan Cohen's study of Mods and Rockers in the mid-1960s. He argued that the media labelled youth culture in a stereotyped and negative way, thus creating "folk devils". These "devils" and their activities were reported in such a way as to create "moral panic". Moral panic occurs when...

"a condition, episode, person or group of persons emerges to become defined as a threat to societal values and interests".

What are you rebelling against, Johnny?

What have you got?

Youth Culture Coverage

Cohen argued that the media's role in structuring public awareness was vitally important. By amplifying the problem, the media created a social reaction against the Mods and Rockers. It galvanized public awareness and police activity. The exaggerated facts scared the public and led the courts to take unusually tough action. A reprehensible and escalating spiral was set in motion, which bore little relation to the real situation.

Don't forget... Mind how you go.

Moral panics also have interesting side effects.

DUMPH!
DUMPH!
DUMPH!
DUMPH!
DUMPH!
DUMPH!
DUMPH!
DUMPH!
DUMPH!
DUMPH!
DUMPH!
DUMPH!
DOOMPH!
DOOMPH!
DOOMPH!
DOOMPH!
DOOMPH!

Without moral panics, many forms of youth culture would never have taken off in the first place. Without such coverage, the "acid house" culture would never have become as popular as it did. The media therefore not only distorts contemporary reality, it can also construct future reality.

Racist ideology

Racial stereotypes are among the most readily employed in the media. The origins of racist ideology lie in colonialism which represented the blacks as "primitive" and "savage" and whites as "civilized" and "developed".

There are three main myths that are "ever-present".

The black person as trouble maker. News items present links between race and crime. Problems are said to be due to the number of immigrants, the influx of refugees, or the cultural identity of the black people.

The black person as entertainer. The classic example of this is the BBC's *Black and White Minstrel Show* (1958–76), in which white male performers put on black face paint and pretended to be black. The high achievers among blacks, both in the United States and Britain, tend to be entertainers – actors, singers, dancers.

The black person as dependent. The famines in Africa portray starving children, and the need for Western intervention to sort things out. More complex causes and effects are brushed aside. These countries therefore appear to lack the competence to be self-sufficient and can only survive with Western support.

Since the 1980s, however, this trend has been slowly changing, with more positive images appearing in the media.

A (token) black character is essential in American TV programmes.

Soap operas have begun to reflect the ethnic diversity of Britain – although even now the Asians always appear as corner shop owners – and ethnic minorities' cultural interests are taken into consideration with programmes on Channel 4 and BBC 2.

The success of the Asian comedy show...

Goodness Gracious Me! ...

is an indication that "black comedy"...

may be moving towards the mainstream.

Representations of Women

Women are constantly portrayed in the media as objects of the male gaze. Semi-naked models are a constant presence on the cover of men's magazines. Bare breasted women (dis)grace most tabloid newspapers. Presenters of popular television programmes are selected for their looks rather than more substantial talent.

One of the most common stereotypes of women is the term "Bimbo". Although this term has a long history dating back at least to the 1920s, it carries particular denigrating connotations in postmodern culture.

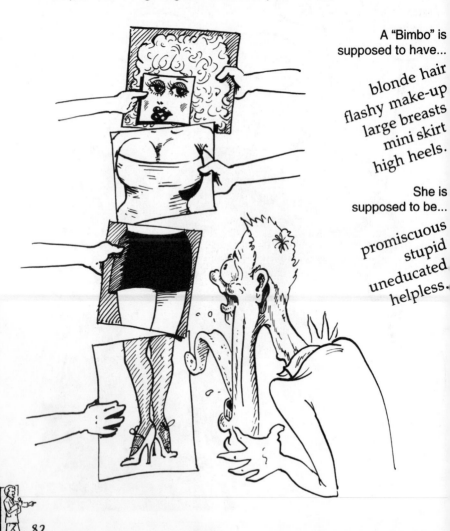

A "Bimbo" is supposed to have...

blonde hair
flashy make-up
large breasts
mini skirt
high heels.

She is supposed to be...

promiscuous
stupid
uneducated
helpless.

And "asking for it" in relation to sexual assault.

The Trouble with Eve

What is highly ironic, although not surprising, is how women themselves inadvertently collude in the manufacture and thus construction of such gender stereotypes. Consider "women's magazines". For the most part, these magazines are written for women by women. But what message are these magazines trying to send out to their readers?

Women's magazines tend to fall into two main categories.
Those concerned with home-making and childcare.
Those aimed at marketing oneself to catch a mate.

This division itself represents the classical dualism of Western thought where a woman is categorized either as

Madonna = pure, maternal, chaste, modest

Or as...

The Whore = loose, sexual, amoral, sinful

Such notions derive in part from Christianity, in which Eve is the source of Original Sin who caused mankind (sic) to be exiled permanently from the Garden of Eden. Her sins were forgiven only after the sacrifice and resurrection of Christ. The idea of the Madonna arises out of the Immaculate Conception and virgin birth of Christ.

Consider the feature headlines in a number of best-selling women's magazines (late summer 1999)

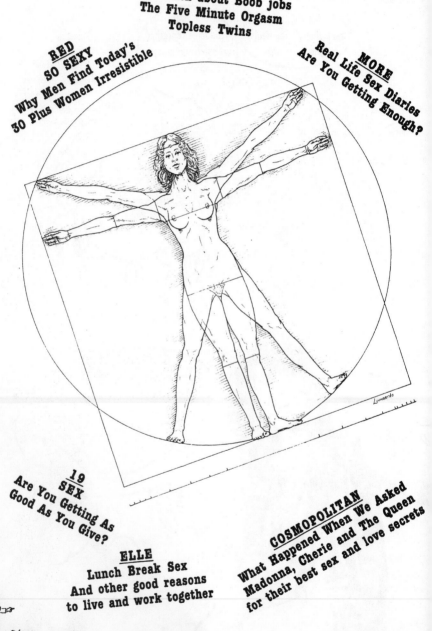

COMPANY
The Truth about Boob jobs
The Five Minute Orgasm
Topless Twins

RED
SO SEXY
Why Men Find Today's
30 Plus Women Irresistible

MORE
Real Life Sex Diaries
Are You Getting Enough?

19
SEX
Are You Getting As
Good As You Give?

ELLE
Lunch Break Sex
And other good reasons
to live and work together

COSMOPOLITAN
What Happened When We Asked
Madonna, Cherie and The Queen
for their best sex and love secrets

The advertising in these magazines is for diet, beauty products and cosmetic surgery, alongside adverts on how to get your whites really white, products for "designer" children and homemaking tips. Plus those mouth-watering recipes which rest on the notion that the way to a man's heart is through his stomach – if the stockings, false eyelashes and Wonderbra fail!

Now, ladies. What better to tempt our menfolk than a nice, spicy tart?

Glossy women's magazines manipulate their readers in highly sophisticated ways. Consider, for example, the images of models that saturate such magazines. The model is photographed lounging in a tight pantsuit wearing high heel boots with locks of shiny hair tumbling over her face and shoulders.

Lawks!

She is looking directly at the camera and her lips are slightly parted, revealing her teeth. Although this photograph is likely to appear as a cover on a women's glossy magazine, it will be digitally altered in ways which appeal to male ideas of female attraction.

87

The pupils of the model's eyes will be altered to appear dilated and thus suggest sexual arousal, the irises made more blue to suggest innocence, the cheeks more flushed to indicate youth as well as sexual arousal, the lips more red to suggest similarities with female genitalia. Of course, any spots, pimples or wrinkles will be removed. The teeth will be whitened to suggest youth and health. Bosoms will be enlarged for obvious reasons.

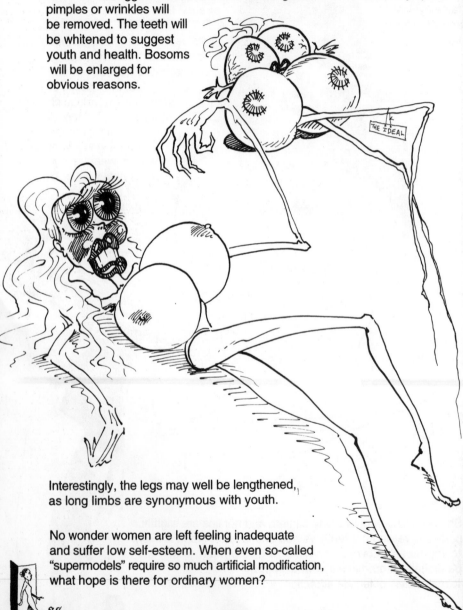

THE IDEAL

Interestingly, the legs may well be lengthened, as long limbs are synonymous with youth.

No wonder women are left feeling inadequate and suffer low self-esteem. When even so-called "supermodels" require so much artificial modification, what hope is there for ordinary women?

NEWS

DOG BITES MAN

That's boring and commonplace.

MAN BITES DOG!

That's news!

This has been the traditional definition of news. An alternative definition suggests that news is the answer to the questions: who, what, where, when, and how.

> But there is more to news than that!

> News is new information on a subject of interest to the recipient. All cleverer and more sententious definitions reveal the preoccupations of their authors.

Ian Hargreaves, former editor of *The Independent* and *New Statesman,* and Professor of Journalism, Cardiff University.

89

Dr Samuel Johnson's (1709-1784) view...

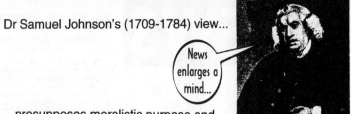

News enlarges a mind...

...presupposes moralistic purpose and a highly selective view of what may legitimately be considered news. The famous notion that news is what is on a society's mind describes only the outlook of certain types of newspaper in certain countries in a particular period.

I would say that news is what somebody, somewhere wants to suppress – all the rest is advertising.

This is pleasingly heroic, but ignores the fact that much news, such as the price of cattle at auction, is both useful and uncontroversial.

News is not an abstract or self-sufficient concept. It exists in relation to other factors. The most important factors are the notions of the "news story" and "news value".

The story and its value

The story is the basic unit in which news is handled. A "good story" has an easy to understand dynamic and, most important of all, closure. It has a beginning, a middle, but also an end, a punch line, a conclusion.

Thus, something that is deemed important on many other criteria may fail to qualify as a story; and not get attention because it is too open ended to make a satisfying story.

"News value" plays an important part in what is seen and selected as a news story. The many criteria that go into the construction of news value have to do with dominant ideas about how society operates, what is seen as important, and what is considered to be of interest to the audience. In general, news value is influenced by the following criteria.

Criteria of News Value

1. **Agenda setting**: the need to tie up news with political agenda and the pressure to manufacture social issues. Even "established facts" are filtered through a number of processes. Facts and impartiality are always at loggerheads with ideology. Most newspapers present their "facts" through their chosen political filters. Transparency is often pitted against constructivism: "facts" can be constructed or manufactured. By taking advantage of its supposedly neutral stance, the media creates consensus in a class-ridden society and sets the agenda on which issues are debated and discussed. For example, it will endorse a two-party parliamentary system by producing a "balance" in the news – reporting the "two sides" of the story – which suggests that the truth must lie somewhere in between. Issues are therefore always debated within certain boundaries.

A POLITICIAN   ANOTHER POLITICIAN   YET ANOTHER POLITICIAN   A TOKEN WOMAN

2. Economic concerns

The media is always concerned with maximizing audiences. A "good" story keeps the reader or viewer interested. Hence, there is great pressure for "Scoops" and "Exclusives". Readers' prejudices and interests are pampered at the expense of Third World issues which are being increasingly neglected. The old adage – one dead in central London is of more interest than 100 dead in South America – is now the norm.

A famine does not exist unless a BBC reporter stumbles upon it.

So... You're poor, hungry, homeless, helpless and destitute... How do you feel?

A great deal of news is also presented as "Infotainment". News programmes tend towards a "show" format, with a "personality" reading the news. The pressure for ratings, and demands of the sponsors and advertisers, often dictate the format and scheduling of news programmes on television.

3. **Immediacy**. Reporters constantly work against deadlines. The pressure for immediacy often forces them to rely on pressure-group spokespersons in order to fill the slot, or "expert opinion" to explain or flesh out an issue. The media nevertheless retain complete control over which experts are actually deemed to be appropriate.

The selection often has more to do with facility within the medium ("presentability" and such like) than with expertise. Immediacy has also led to 24-hour news services such as CNN, Sky News and BBC News 24, which report news "as it happens".

4. Gate-keeping. The whole process of choosing or rejecting stories on the basis of news value is called "gate-keeping". The gate-keeping role is performed largely by editors, including those who oversee particular sections of the newspapers. In television, this role is sometimes taken by producers and executive producers.

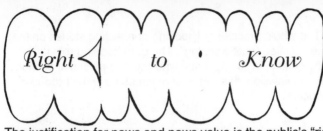

Right to Know

The justification for news and news value is the public's "right to know", a concept that functions on principles enshrined in law that supposedly govern the operation of reporters. These principles are exemplified by America's First Amendment rights and the constitutional protections of the British system. The media is *de facto* the eyes and ears of the public within the system of governance and operation of the courts of law.

So long as the press is present, the public is deemed to be in attendance.

This has come to be understood as a need to service the requirements of the press – for instance, with regular press briefings, or the system of embargoed notice to the press of forthcoming events. The system builds close relations between the press and established centres of power and influence.

War Reporting

In times of crisis, the press often becomes an agency of government, as in the case of war reporting. This dynamic was unquestioned during the Second World War but has come under much closer scrutiny in the post-Vietnam era, largely as a result of the dissonance between what the American government had to say about the war in Vietnam and what reporters of the first television war actually saw and reported.

Another war! More work for Adie!

Now war is cued on TV. One knows when war is likely to happen because Kate Adie of the BBC wears a combat jacket and Christiane Amanpour of CNN appears on a rooftop!

Investigative Reporting

Investigative reporting is the press operating its alternate interpretation of the public's "right to know" to uncover what officialdom does not wish to make public. The investigative function is used as a justification for special freedoms, authority and moral acumen by the media, claims which do not always stand up to scrutiny. The Watergate Investigation is part of the myth and ethos of the news media.

But it can be argued that the success of that investigation has created a pattern of media behaviour that sees character and personal lives as the only issue worthy of attention, particularly in American presidential campaigns.

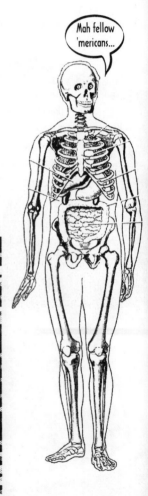

Mah fellow 'mericans...

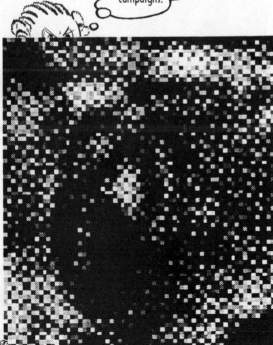

BA**D NE**WS

War reporting has been extensively analysed by the Glasgow University Media Group (GUMG). The Group's reports, *Bad News* (1980) and *More Bad News* (1985), are considered a milestone in media analysis.

In their analysis of the Falklands War in 1982, GUMG showed that four filtering processes affected the news.

1. Time, resources, geography.
2. News value.
3. The notion of "good television".
4. The need to confirm the views of the "ordinary man"; thus implicitly affirming the status quo.

In the course of their work, GUMG were no strangers to hostility from both BBC and ITN.

la fin du voyage.

99

In their analysis of the Gulf War in 1991, GUMG showed that the media tended to portray the inevitability of war and emphasize a clear, clean and easy war.

John Simpson, BBC World Affairs Editor*:

Comics

Newspapers first started to carry comic strips at the turn of the century. But it was not until *Superman* made an appearance in June 1938 that the comic book really came into its own. Superheroes proliferated and found instant rapport with young Americans. During the 1950s new genres were developed: the *Classics* series which illustrated Great Literature...

...and Horror Comics which battled with the censors.

Real anarchist breakthroughs arrived in the 1960s with <u>Mad</u> comics...

...and underground satire, while superheroes matured in complexity with *Spider-Man*, *The Fantastic Four* and others. American comics tended to reinforce the Cold War themes of anti-Communist paranoia and "alien invasion", but also counter-culture protest. British comics like *Beano* and *Dandy* instead related the exploits of naughty boys (and sometimes girls) and football heroes. These were aimed squarely at eight- to twelve-year-olds, printed on cheap paper and designed to be thrown away after a single read.

BAH!

In 1988, Superman turned 50. Comics came of age. By now, they had broken into film, television and animation.

Hah! nearly drawing his pension, eh?

Genres of Comics

STRIPS!

GRAPHIC NOVELS!

COMIC BOOKS!

The Author...

And, let us be a little self-referential: the Comic Book Study Guides, of which the **Introducing** series is a good – indeed, the only – example!

The Illustrator...

Here, you can see all the tricks of the trade from balloons and motion lines to sound effects!

—HOLY SHIT!

BIFF!

KRAK!

POW!

Animation

Animation is a natural progression from comics. It dates back to the early 20th century, but it was not until the 1930s, when sound and colour emerged, that animation became popular.

Looks like a hurricane to me!

The early pioneers discovered the golden formula for producing the illusion of smooth, natural motion: **24 frames per second.**

Flick the top right hand corner of this book and see!

For every second of movement, we need to photograph 24 different frames or "cells".

Thus, a ten minute *Donald Duck* cartoon contains 14,400 cells.

An average episode of *The Simpsons*, which lasts only 22 minutes, contains 31,680 cells.

In the 1950s and 60s, Hanna-Barbera cartoons dominated TV screens. Shows like *Quick Draw McGraw*, *Yogi Bear* and *The Jetsons* used formulaic plots and two-dimensional characters, and were cheaper to produce than Disney products.

Disney developed a visual imagery for its animation that relied on live action conventions. Disney offered classic realist narrative, three-dimensional characterization and movement, and such film techniques as depth shots, pans and zooms. Disney animation can be divided into two trends: the graphic-like simplicity of films like *Dumbo* and the detailed naturalism of *Bambi*.

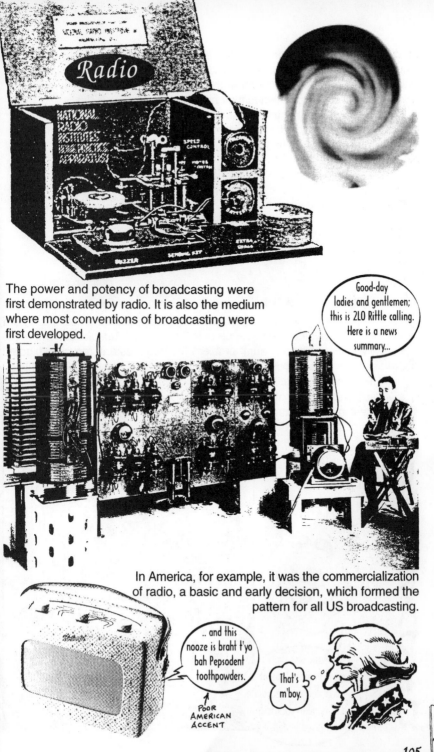

The power and potency of broadcasting were first demonstrated by radio. It is also the medium where most conventions of broadcasting were first developed.

Good-day ladies and gentlemen; this is 2LO Rittle calling. Here is a news summary...

In America, for example, it was the commercialization of radio, a basic and early decision, which formed the pattern for all US broadcasting.

.. and this nooze is braht t'yo bah Pepsodent toothpowders.

POOR AMERICAN ACCENT

That's m'boy.

Radio is cheap, easy to produce and allows more effective public access. This creates tremendous power for radio that can be utilized for social and economic development. A strength that was used most notably by the Sandinistas in Nicaragua during their bitter struggles against the US-supported "Contras" in a civil war that lasted nearly ten years to 1989.

DOWNMARKETING RADIO

Radio thrives on niche markets but suffers more noticeably from trivialization because of it. Sensational "tabloid talk" radio, the voyeurism of "agony aunt" problem programmes and recycling bigoted personal opinion as so-called "access" are notable examples. Fragmentation of the audience is also at its highest in radio because of the facility of the technology.

Music was the most popular type of programming on early radio, and it remains such today, followed by talk.

Advertising ....

...exists to create

DESIRE.

Like film and television, ads are "texts" that can be deciphered. But they are highly condensed texts directed solely at making an emotional impact.

Advertising has now become an integral part of our culture.

An individual of 60 years of age has seen, heard or read over 50 million advertisements!

Even the election of politicians, especially US presidents, is now determined by advertising. Governments now spend more money on advertisements that promote their policies than do multinationals.

OH MY GOD I BUY!!!
CHARGE IT!
CONSUME
I WANT IT & I MUST HAVE IT
GIMME GIMME
EAT GORGE GIM
I WANT
LORD SAVE ME FROM WHAT I WANT
BUY
SPEND SPEND SPEND
GRAB CREDIT CARD OK?
BUY IT NOW!
GOBBLE BUY BUY
WANT IT NOW!
WILL YOU TAKE A CHEQUE?
NOW NOW NOW NOW
SLAVER!
PUT IT ON MY BILL
BLIMEY, I FORGOT TO GET DRESSED
I WANT IT
I BUY BUY BUY
GIVE IT TO ME
I WANT IT NOW!
NOW!
I DON'T DESIRE IT I MUST HAVE IT!
I WANT IT & I WANT IT NOW!

107

Everything FOR SALE

Advertising readily borrows from TV, film and other media. Ads can be presented as "news", as a mini-documentary and even a soap opera. Examples are the long-running "soap opera" campaigns on British TV for Nescafé Gold Blend or the OXO family story.

The logical end point is the "infomercial", an extended advert that purports to be a documentary or a chat show. It is a genre of advertising born entirely out of mainstream TV that blurs all standards and genres. But it does make it evident that **all** media are selling something, whether ideas, lifestyle choices or views on the nature of existence!

Ad Formats

Postmodern advertisements can be very sophisticated and stuffed with "intertextual" references. Some, like the ad for Silk Cut cigarettes, don't even seem to be selling anything. Others imply signs and symbols from totally different texts, sources and styles – like the mobile phone ad that presents itself as a "revolution" and exploits the iconic symbols of the Bolshevik revolution.

WARNING: Smoking may slightly damage your health

In general, advertisements follow four standard formats.

Product-information format – in which the product is the centre of the focus and its virtues are pointed out and explained.

Product-image format – in which the product is associated with certain images that we may not readily attribute to it. For example, a cigarette burning at several hundred degrees with a cool mountain stream!

Personalized format – in which a direct relationship is established between the product and the human personality. The product is presented as an intimate partner, and takes on human qualities.

Lifestyle format – in which the product is associated with a particular lifestyle. Very popular with soft drink, car and mobile phone ads.

Ad Techniques

Advertising uses a number of techniques to fool us.

<u>The weasel words technique</u> where empty but colourful words –
new, improved, helps, refreshes, fights, whiter –
are used.

Washes whiter than white.

<u>The endorsement technique</u> where a (vacuous) celebrity tells us how wonderful the product is.

As a footballer I need to have my teeth shining white. So I use Shit Toothpaste. It helps fight tooth decay and keeps me smiling.

<u>The statistical technique</u> which claims to provide statistical proof of the product.

Nine out of ten cats prefer Kattomeat.

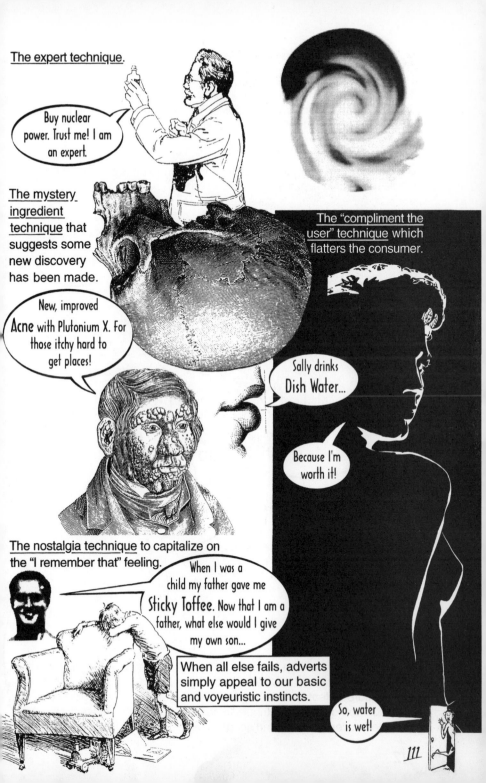

Television

Television was unleashed in 1939. Sixty years on, it has conquered the world. Only the tiny, devoutly Buddhist, Bhutan refused to fall to the charms of television. But, in 1999, it too relented and allowed television into the country for the first time.

Bhutan now provides ideal conditions in which to answer a number of key media research questions.

Is television good or bad for society? Is watching television simply a harmless pastime or does it lead to the "dumbing down" of society? Is society more violent because of violent programmes on television? Does television pornography contribute to sexism in society? Do lifestyles promoted in certain American soaps lead to conspicuous consumption?

Media research has failed to give satisfactory answers to these and other similar questions. Perhaps, in time Bhutan may provide a clear answer to whether or not the media in general, and television in particular, carry perverse influences.

Meanwhile, the rest of the world has buried itself in the following genres of television.

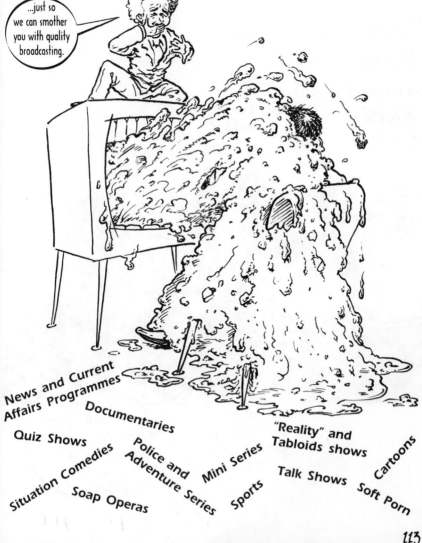

News and Current Affairs Programmes

Documentaries

Quiz Shows

"Reality" and Tabloids shows

Cartoons

Situation Comedies

Police and Adventure Series

Mini Series

Talk Shows

Soft Porn

Soap Operas

Sports

Television Production

Each stage of television production, from initial idea to the final transmission of a programme, involves decision-making, interpretation, constraints, flexibility and continuous **negotiation**.

All programmes begin with an idea. Given that networks are becoming more like publishing houses, commissioning and buying programmes from independent production companies, ideas are just as likely to come from outside the organizations as within them.

This "bidding process" can considerably alter the initial idea and story line. The idea is subjected to scrutiny at each level of television hierarchy from the Director General (or equivalent) to executive producers, editors, producers, associate producers, right down to the lowly researcher.

So you go in with a neat pitch about making Shakespeare for the masses and end up with a soap opera!

I would never have taken the part in this book if I'd known it was going to be so small.

Prithee, mistress, wilt thou accompany your humble servant for refreshment at a nearby coffee-house, forsooth?

Prithee, sirrah, stand not on the order of thy going, but sling your 'ook.

I get this feeling of déjà vu.

In publishing it's called economy.

Once an idea has been accepted, and budgets have been allocated, the production process begins.

The Building Blocks of Production

The production process is divided into three parts – pre-production, filming (the term is used even if the technical medium is video) and post-production.

Pre-production

The pre-production work depends on whether it is a studio-based or a fixed location production, or an outside broadcast, or a documentary, or a feature film involving location filming.

Studio-based production needs lighting, camera, sound and recording infrastructure, and a whole army of people – studio directors, production assistants, vision mixers, floor managers, set designers and autocue folks. Studio facilities can vary from the large studio complexes that house drama productions…

Fixed location. This could be the theatre from which a chat show with a live audience is broadcast, or the historic castle that is the main location for a costume drama.

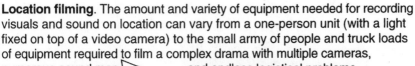

Outside broadcast. The term is applied to relaying an actual event such as a sporting occasion or a parade. But the resources that enable these transmissions can also be used to produce other kinds of programming, such as sheepdog trials or a road show, in which a format programme goes out to meet its audience.

Location filming. The amount and variety of equipment needed for recording visuals and sound on location can vary from a one-person unit (with a light fixed on top of a video camera) to the small army of people and truck loads of equipment required to film a complex drama with multiple cameras, numerous sound men and endless logistical problems.

Research. All production requires research. On a studio-based game show, for example, contestants must be found, questions and answers must be checked. Graphics, set design, costumes all may require research. In documentaries, research needs to be done to find participants and locations. Research includes all of the logistics support, from how to get location catering to the top of a mountain to ensuring that parking permission has been granted for the crew to unload their equipment, let alone the various permissions necessary to film in a public place.

Pre-film script. In drama and feature films, the script is worked out well in advance. In documentaries and current affairs programmes, a pre-film script – giving a good idea of what is to be filmed where, and who is going to say what – is prepared.

Filming

During filming, any programme idea – no matter how exact the pre-film script – is subjected to a whole variety of circumstances that can affect the final outcome. The purpose of filming is to render an approximation of actuality in an interesting and visually pleasing way. Even with gritty documentaries, this means recreating reality, breaking it down into pieces of action that are separately recorded and cut together at a later stage.

Documentaries recreate everyday action and make it look as if the camera was not present.

The more ordinary the participants, the more scope there is for a documentary crew to get them to spend hours recreating actuality with endless patience, while their home is turned upside down.

Post-production

Post-production begins with editing. Video editing is a lot less tactile and pleasing than film editing, and those reared on film editing often criticize video editing for being "less sensitive". Big video-editing suites are expensive, but cheap pre-edit, offline editing equipment is often used to experiment and prepare an editing script.

The initial idea can undergo enormous changes during editing. A strong visual sequence, even one that is tangential and unplanned, can affect how a programme is put together and the message(s) it carries.

Editing is not merely a process of compiling the pieces of action into a coherent story. It is also the assemblage of actuality recorded at different times, in different places, with different people, into one coherent story.

Further juxtapositions are created by including archive footage, stills and graphics, and the texture and look of these can be affected by the whole array of editing effects and video effects now available.

It is at the editing stage that a programme is most likely to re-enter the scrutiny of the decision-making hierarchy. The editing period is a major occasion for negotiation, during which influence can be brought to bear on what story is told, how it is told, and what messages it will contain. It is axiomatic that any material entering an editing process can end up making a number of different programmes. The editing process refines the story that will be told out of the many other potential ones.

A controversial programme may have to satisfy everyone, being re-edited a number of times before transmission.

Once the programme is edited, it may then be subject to scripting. And the final script may be the result of many influences and rewrites. The process of scripting, writing just the right three words per second, picking up on what the pictures say without merely telling what can already be seen, is a skilled art form. The narrated script can dramatically affect a programme.

The End Result

The final stage of post-production is dubbing. The sound track of the programme is finally assembled and script narration recorded.

Music is added to enhance dramatic effects.

Television programmes, especially documentaries, are made in pre-production research and planning, remade during filming, and remade again during post-production. The initial story may only ever be approximated. What will matter at the end of the day is the story that is broadcast, its credibility and ability to generate, hold and please an audience. Good visuals always win out over strong ideas.

ARGUMENTS AGAINST TELEVISION

Excessive television watching, it has been argued, is …

Public Service Broadcasting

Public service broadcasting is seen either as a dinosaur trying to exist after the meteor has landed, or as the last best hope for freedom of expression.

The oldest public broadcasting service in the world is the BBC. It began (radio) broadcasting in 1922. Under the guiding spirit of Sir John Reith, it established the mantra for media public service in the famous catchphrase …

To educate, inform and entertain.

Its aim was to perform these functions without political interference, with objectivity and editorial independence. What made the independent Corporation possible was a licence fee levied on the ownership of a radio set, and later a television set.

There was a brief moment of discussion of the public service model when radio first emerged in the US. This quickly succumbed to the ethos of the market. But it re-emerged in the 1970s when PBS, the Public Broadcasting Service, was established as a non-profit, non-commercial chain of broadcasting stations.

The arguments for and against public service broadcasting are not merely about means of funding.

> Broadcasting paid for by advertising is _not_ free to the public. It is paid for in the price of goods and services purchased by all consumers.

> Oh no! We're missing Dixon of Dock Green.

Paying a licence fee may make broadcasters notionally more responsive to their audience and its preferences, but advertisers may have more direct influence on programming choices and content than an unorganized general public.

Quality is the Thing

The real argument is supposedly about quality of programming, content and diversity. It is generally assumed that …

COMMERCIAL BROADCASTING = *ENTERTAINMENT-DRIVEN, LOWEST COMMON DENOMINATOR SERVICE.*

PUBLIC SERVICE = *QUALITY PROGRAMMING AND CATERING TO MINORITY AUDIENCES WITH A WIDE DIVERSITY OF PROGRAMME TYPES AND CONTENT.*

The dichotomy is less clear than its proponents claim.

Nothing on the telly tonight. Let's go down the pub.

I'll get me coat...

To justify their existence, public service broadcasters also have to be entertainment-driven and ratings-obsessed. When broadcasting hours and channels are limited, the mass audience always dominates over minorities and special interest audiences. Despite the myth that the BBC produces quality programmes, it has, during the 1990s, subsided into junk television.

FILM FLM FM

Film is one of the commonest and most widespread sources of entertainment. The film industry is a global conglomerate of capital, as well as a cultural influence and power.

But movies are much more than entertainment. Films are again "texts" with encoded meanings which can be read. They use **indexical**, **iconic** and **symbolic** devices, which are readily identified by audiences. Indeed, cinema uses signifiers as a shorthand to help propel the narrative flow. So, for example, in *Don't Look Now* (1973) red is a constant **signifier** which connotes passion, death, danger and hidden tensions. It becomes the central motif of the movie. In *The Maltese Falcon* (1931), the statue of the falcon is an **iconic signifier**. Shots of the White House, signifying the American government, or of the Statue of Liberty or the Eiffel Tower, standing for a geographical place or locating the narrative, are commonly used in films as **metonymic signifiers**. Symbolic signs, such as dark shadows, snow and gothic sets are used to denote peril or purity or suspense. Smoke, sweat or skin eruptions are used as **indexical signs** to connote fire, effort or plague. Films also rely on **intertextuality**: thus, one film may make a reference to another, either explicitly by dialogue or implicitly by stealing the sequence – for example, the Odessa Steps sequence from *Battleship Potemkin* (1925) relocated to Grand Central Station in the remake of *The Untouchables* (1987).

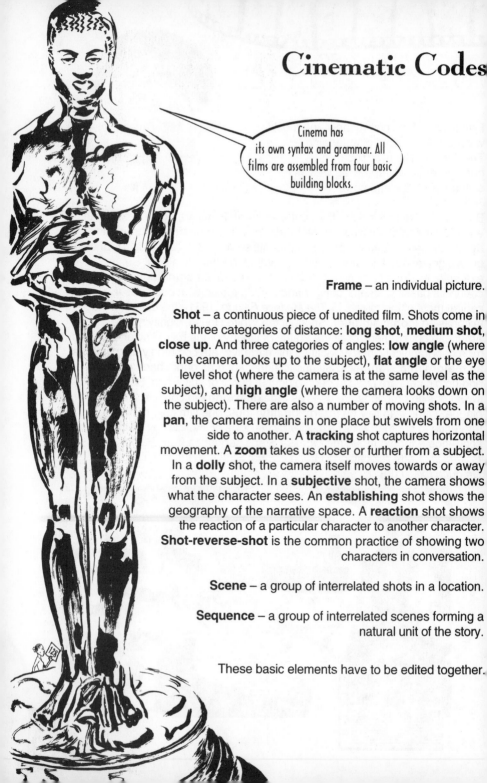

Cinematic Codes

Cinema has its own syntax and grammar. All films are assembled from four basic building blocks.

Frame – an individual picture.

Shot – a continuous piece of unedited film. Shots come in three categories of distance: **long shot**, **medium shot**, **close up**. And three categories of angles: **low angle** (where the camera looks up to the subject), **flat angle** or the eye level shot (where the camera is at the same level as the subject), and **high angle** (where the camera looks down on the subject). There are also a number of moving shots. In a **pan**, the camera remains in one place but swivels from one side to another. A **tracking** shot captures horizontal movement. A **zoom** takes us closer or further from a subject. In a **dolly** shot, the camera itself moves towards or away from the subject. In a **subjective** shot, the camera shows what the character sees. An **establishing** shot shows the geography of the narrative space. A **reaction** shot shows the reaction of a particular character to another character. **Shot-reverse-shot** is the common practice of showing two characters in conversation.

Scene – a group of interrelated shots in a location.

Sequence – a group of interrelated scenes forming a natural unit of the story.

These basic elements have to be edited together.

Early Hollywood produced the Hayes code, a set of conventions to control the sexual and moral content of film imagery. Kisses were timed and double beds never appeared. Today, however, anything goes!

129

Editing

Just like TV programmes, films can be made and remade by editing.

The most simple form is **real time** editing, in which the time taken by the sequence is equal to the time of the performance.

Continuity editing ensures that different parts of the sequence naturally integrate together (characters do not jump out of place, for example, or change in any unintended way). It is the basic tool for disguising the artificial construction of the narrative.

Montage involves juxtaposing contrasting shots to create meaning. Each edit proceeds justifiably from one shot to another – for example, the shot of a gun firing can lead naturally to a close up of the gun.

Fading in and out is a common technique for showing the passage of time. **Flashback**, which may involve fading in and out, is a standard technique for relating past events.

The **180 degree rule** ensures that the camera tends to stay on one side of an imaginary 180 degree line of action which can be drawn through any scene, for example a car chase or a conversation between two people. Breaking the rule gives the impression that the characters have changed position.

Reading Film

A movie can be divided into three general and often overlapping constituents, the basic ingredients of a story: plot, narrative, theme. Lets look at these ingredients with the example of *Independence Day* (*ID*), the blockbuster movie of 1997.

Plot

This is the easiest to grasp. It is the synopsis of the story, which also tells us the **genre** of the film.

POWERFUL ALIENS LAUNCH AN INVASION OF PLANET EARTH

Don't worry – he's only playing.

Look, piss off. OK?

132

Against terrifying and incalculable odds, a few brave men, aided by the genius of an expert, foil an alien invasion and save the human race.

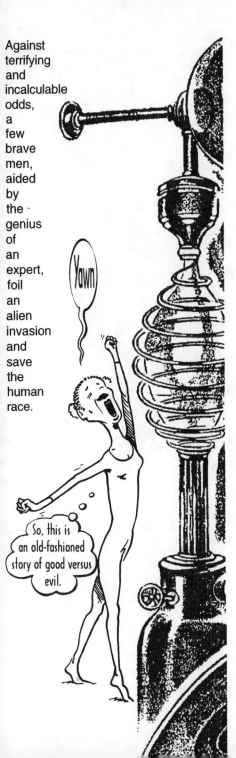

Yawn

So, this is an old-fashioned story of good versus evil.

But there are also sub-plots which reveal more about the film. Hollywood cinema reflects the psychological, political and economic concerns of American society. This is particularly evident in the science fiction genre. *Independence Day* draws its inspiration from classic sci-fi B-movies from the 1950s, such as *Invasion of the Bodysnatchers* (1956), *War of the Worlds* (1953) and *Invaders From Mars* (1953). These movies actually functioned as Cold War metaphors which expressed American paranoid fears of Communism, totalitarian regimes and nuclear war.

The idea of an alien or extra-terrestrial becomes the focus of these fears – Commies as "little green men".

133

Alien Angst

A Big Mac and Coke it surely aint!

ID mobilizes the cultural metaphor of the "alien" to reflect American fears of difference – in particular, fear of non-Western cultures which are perceived as a threat to the American dream of global dominance. We can see the plot of *ID* as a manifesto for American foreign policy, that is, as the only rational response of a civilized nation in the face of international conflict. American military presence in the Gulf or in Bosnia is symbolically vindicated by films like *ID*.

A further sub-plot cashes in on "millennium angst". The decline of faith in the secularized West has engendered the search for meaning beyond the notion of an omnipresent God. We end up with a collective hallucination saturated with narratives of UFOs, alien visitors and alien abductees, government cover-ups, CIA conspiracies, the fear of approaching Armageddon – the kind of paranoia reflected so well in the *The X-Files*. *ID* exploits these fears and uncertainties, its apocalyptic doomsday overtones echoing the prophecies currently circulating throughout the globe.

The Narrative of *ID*

Woven together, the plot and sub-plots frame the narrative of the movie.

The surface narrative of ID suggests a politically correct movie.

It has people of colour, a gay character, a child and even a dog!

What do you mean: even a dog?

There are two leading characters: David Levinson (Jeff Goldblum) and Captain Steve Hiller (Will Smith).

Levinson has all the trappings of the archetypal "new man". He dresses casually, appears vulnerable and sensitive, and is over-protective of his stereotypical Jewish father. He is also a cybergenius, and his obvious intelligence and moral authority are underlined by the prop of tortoise-shell glasses.

Levinson has been abandoned by his wife, who has sacrificed her marriage to become the right-hand person of the President.

Levinson discovers a way of neutralizing the alien crafts. President Whitmore pilots the plane that leads the charge against the aliens.

OK, guys. Let's go and beat the crap out of some aliens.

The aliens are defeated and the earth reverberates with the sounds of humanity surviving against all odds.

CRIKEY! (IN MY ALIEN VOICE)

Theme

The plot and the narrative expose the theme of a movie.

Ostensibly, *ID*'s theme focusses on human triumph in the face of adversity: a quest for human dignity in an undignified world. But if we stop here, we would have failed to read the film.

The characters themselves convey hidden messages. Both Captain Hiller and Jasmine are presented as stereotypical blacks. His semi-naked body, sexualized and objectified, transports us back in time to the "Noble Savage" and the "White Man's Burden". He may well fight to liberate humanity from the alien menace, but he is still black. He is much more expendable as fodder for Uncle Sam's clarion call to fight for the flag. We get to see Jasmine strip. This functions both as titillation for the male audience and to remind the female audience of their objectified status.

Levinson may be a Renaissance man – but boy, he still doesn't get the girl! Only by transforming himself into a knight in shining armour and slaying the "dragon" (the alien mother ship) can he win back the love of his woman. He is little more than a male heterosexual fantasy disguised as the feminist ideal. And the message is clear. To be happy, all women need is to be put firmly back in their "place" via a good dose of machismo.

The Rightful Place for Women

In contrast to Jasmine's fallen woman, we have the Madonna-like qualities of the First Lady, Patricia. As a single mother, Jasmine is a threat to the wholesomeness of American family values. The only path to redemption for her "sinful" ways is to be upgraded to an honourable married woman. Patricia's role is to remind the audience of men's (God's) natural intended "rightful place for women": raising beautiful children and dutifully supporting the more "important" work of men. Even in death, her dignity and helplessness further serve to remind us that women ought to be stoical and accepting, suffering their fate in silence.

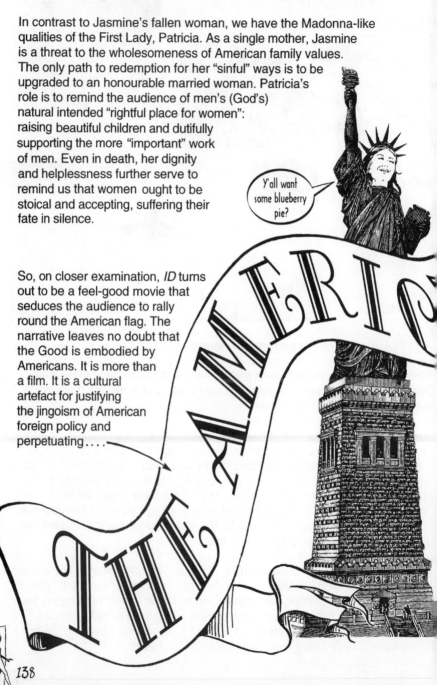

Y'all want some blueberry pie?

So, on closer examination, *ID* turns out to be a feel-good movie that seduces the audience to rally round the American flag. The narrative leaves no doubt that the Good is embodied by Americans. It is more than a film. It is a cultural artefact for justifying the jingoism of American foreign policy and perpetuating . . . .

THE AMERICA

HOLLYWOOD and IN DREAM INDUSTRY

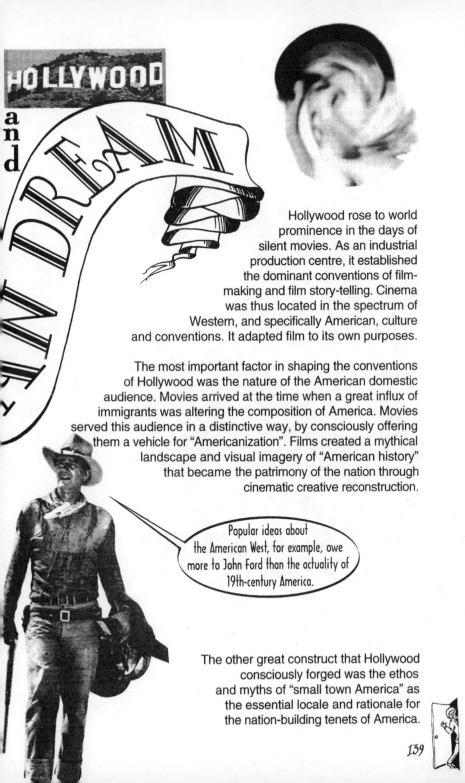

Hollywood rose to world prominence in the days of silent movies. As an industrial production centre, it established the dominant conventions of film-making and film story-telling. Cinema was thus located in the spectrum of Western, and specifically American, culture and conventions. It adapted film to its own purposes.

The most important factor in shaping the conventions of Hollywood was the nature of the American domestic audience. Movies arrived at the time when a great influx of immigrants was altering the composition of America. Movies served this audience in a distinctive way, by consciously offering them a vehicle for "Americanization". Films created a mythical landscape and visual imagery of "American history" that became the patrimony of the nation through cinematic creative reconstruction.

Popular ideas about the American West, for example, owe more to John Ford than the actuality of 19th-century America.

The other great construct that Hollywood consciously forged was the ethos and myths of "small town America" as the essential locale and rationale for the nation-building tenets of America.

139

Hollywood Stereotypes

The hero motif became a staple of the Hollywood system. Colonialism and racism were central props of its story-telling. The stereotypes of "the Other" – the black, the Native American, the Oriental – that Hollywood continually recycles, took their place alongside the evil industrialists, the noble homesteader, the Latin lover and the Italian-American gangster.

Hollywood is not only referential to the products of Western "high culture", but also to all the genres of popular culture. And it has become increasingly **self**-referential, acknowledging its own importance within the culture of America. Films such as the *Indiana Jones* series are pastiches of 1930s and 40s films. Popular television series become the basis of films, such as the *Brady Bunch* movies. Comic-book superheroes such as *Batman* (1989) and *The Phantom* (1996) are made into "real-life" movie heroes. Animation now spawns real-life recycling such as *The Flintstones* (1994) and *101 Dalmatians* (1997).

Hollywood's Global Market

The vast spending power of Asian audiences now has considerable impact on Hollywood output.

It drives the production of hero tales that are long on action, short on script, and laden with special effects. The relationship of Hollywood to its global market is interactive. It commands audience loyalty because of American economic and political power. It offers the world a particular perspective on the obsessions, desires, fashions and trends of contemporary America.

It serves as a global guide to would-be modernizers seeking to domesticate this affluent modernity within their own lifestyles.

And, of course, Hollywood is the hub of global production of icons and images.

World Cinema: Bollywood

While Hollywood is still one of the most prolific producers of film, it is eclipsed in terms of sheer output by Bollywood cinema, the major producer of Hindi and Urdu films, situated in the Indian city of Bombay, now renamed Mumbai. But big film industries also exist in Hong Kong and China, Japan and Egypt. In comparison, Australia and European countries – France, Britain, Sweden, Germany, Italy – have a relatively low output. Some countries, such as Iran and Guinea Bissau, have thriving art film industries.

Bollywood has pioneered the unique genre of squeezing many different kinds of film into a single three-hour movie – a composite of all-singing, all-dancing, all-action, comedy, tragedy, family movie. Contemporary Indian films are noted for their spectacular song and dance routines. The music video, as we know it today, has its origins in the Indian cinema.

Some of the great films of Indian cinema have been produced in this genre. Typical films of the celebrated thespian **Dilip Kumar** (b. 1922), *Mughal-e-Azam* (1960) and *Ganga Jumna* (1961), transform the formula into high art. Others have achieved artistic merit by breaking the mould – most notably **Satyajit Ray** (1921–92), with films like *Pather Panchali* (1955) and *The*

Hong Kong Cinema

吳宇森

梁朝偉、冠華友·李子茲

Woo!

Hong Kong cinema is noted for its action films. Not surprisingly, it is the home of the original Kung Fu movies.

The success of Hong Kong films is reflected in the fact that all Hollywood action heroes now fight like Bruce Lee! And action directors like John Woo are now coveted in Hollywood.

Woo has been described as "the poet of violence". His films *The Killers* (1989) and *A Better Tomorrow* (1986) have legendary reputations.

Hong Kong action actors, such as Jackie Chan and Chow Yun Fat, are now equally at home in Hollywood. Samo Hung stars in the highly-rated CBS television show *Marshall Law*.

144

Samo Hung

Cinema Elsewhere

In many Asian and African countries, films have been used to develop a notion of national identity. In Indonesia, for example, the government used the cinema to construct a discourse on nationalism to mould different ethnicities into a single "nation".

Iranian cinema is known for producing an unusually high number of masterpieces. The post-revolution cinema tends to explore the issues of innocence and authenticity in deceptively simple narratives, frequently playing with the notions of representation, and often employing non-professional actors. Check out films like *The White Balloon* (1995), *Through the Olive Trees* (1994) and *Close-up* (1990).

White Baloon

Third Cinema

Third Cinema is committed to political and cultural liberation. The term should not be confused with "Third World Cinema" (a category in its own right), although for historical reasons Third Cinema first emerged in Latin America in the decade after the 1959 Cuban revolution, which greatly influenced it.

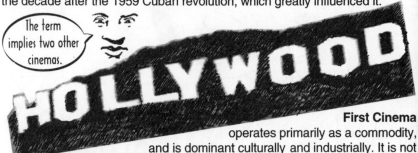

The term implies two other cinemas.

First Cinema operates primarily as a commodity, and is dominant culturally and industrially. It is not homogenous, but from Hollywood to low-budget generic production in Nigeria, it has a certain unity in its characteristics, commercial intentions and mode of address.

Historically, **Second Cinema** emerged as an alternative to First Cinema, emphasizing the importance of national cultural expression from a middle-class perspective. Essentially an **art cinema**, it is committed to the notion of the director's unique artistic vision and sensibility.

ROXY

Third Cinema Season

...st. showing of the big film 9pm

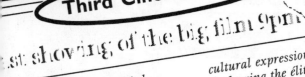

Like First Cinema, Third Cinema seeks to address a popular audience, but as political subjects who are part of historical processes, rather than consumers. Like Second Cinema, Third Cinema places great emphasis on cultural expression and identity. Eschewing the élitism and individualism of Second Cinema, it focusses instead on the hunger for cultural expression of politically marginalized classes and groups.

Michael Wayne,
Lecturer in
Film Studies,
Brunel University

Examples of Third Cinema ...

The Emerald Forest
(USA, 1985)

The Battle of Algiers
(Algeria/France, 1965)

Mapantsula
(South Africa, 1988)

EARTH
(India, 1999)

Indochine
(France, 1991)

Third Cinema can work with different forms of documentary, and across the range of fictional genres. It challenges both the way in which cinema is conventionally made (it has pioneered collective and democratic production methods) and the way in which it is consumed (it refuses to be mere entertainment). Historically, Third Cinema has been a **socialist** cinema opposed to the rule of capital.

Kia-ora and pop-corn on sale inside
(During the interval, Mabel and Dolly will visit all parts of the theatre with drinks on sticks, nuts in bags and ices in wrappers. I thank you.)

147

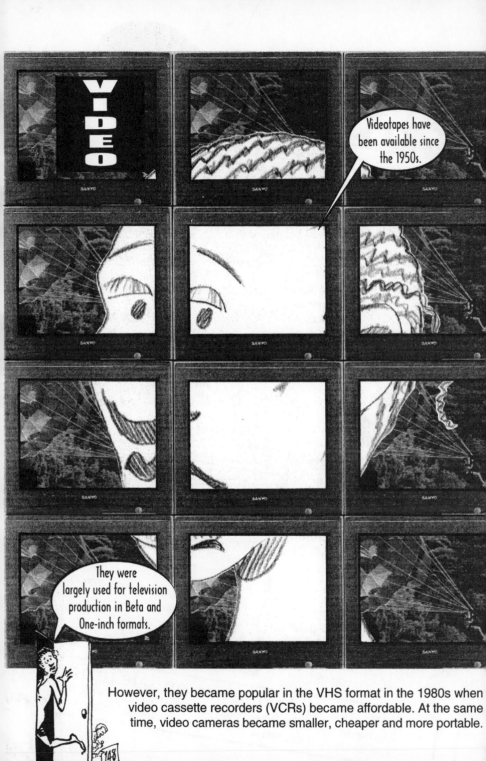

However, they became popular in the VHS format in the 1980s when video cassette recorders (VCRs) became affordable. At the same time, video cameras became smaller, cheaper and more portable.

They were first used in television news-gathering when ENG (electronic news-gathering) crews – in some cases reduced to a single reporter with a camera – became a good way of cutting costs.

VCRs give viewers some control over how they watch a programme.

Using VCRs, viewers can watch shows broadcast simultaneously over competing networks by recording programmes and watching them at their leisure.

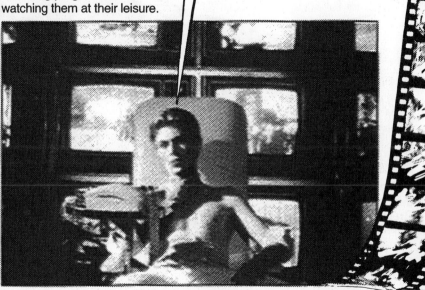

This plays havoc both with carefully planned network schedules and the television rating systems, rendering the concept of "audience share" obsolete. Recorded tapes can also be fast-forwarded to skip advertisements. This has raised the question: should advertisers be compensated for lost airtime?

Videos also give a new lease of life to films. Once their box office revenues begin to dwindle, films are released on video. Some films, deemed uneconomical for theatre release, are released straight to video.

And older movies can now live on the shelves of video stores – instead of disappearing completely from public view.

The music industry in general, and MTV in particular, has used the capabilities of video in innovative ways. Digital effects and mixed-media video editing are staple components of the music video.

149

The Video Revolution

The camcorder has created a revolution in DIY videos. The last decade has seen the emergence of a whole genre of television programmes devoted solely to viewers' "home" videos, such as *You've been Framed* and numerous shows with titles that begin with "America's Worst/Best/…".

Amateur videos also play an important part in the news, as proven in the 1991 video of Los Angeles police beating me, Rodney King, a black "suspect".

AMATEUR VIDEO MAR. 3 1991

RODNEY KING
BEATING VICTIM

Political activists such as Greenpeace and Animal Rights campaigners now routinely record their protests and actions to sell to networks for use in news and current affairs programmes.

The Blair Witch Project, the horror hit of 1999, was shot totally on Hi-8 video by two independent film-makers for $50,000!

That's scary!

Fake Videos

Videos have also generated a whole new culture of fakes. In almost every city of the world, illegally duplicated films can be bought for next to nothing. During the 1980s, illegal duplicating of Bollywood films nearly ruined the Indian film industry.

Fake films come in three basic varieties.

1. The commonest type is the film that has actually been re-filmed. This involves smuggling a Super-8 video camera inside a theatre and recording the proceedings. Invariably, the sound quality is bad, and often you get only part of the film. It does, however, provide you with the postmodern experience of observing the observers, witnessing the audience's reactions and their enjoyment – or not – of the film. One can hear the audience laughing, booing, hissing, gasping with fear or excitement, as well as witness their excursions to buy popcorn or their visits to the toilet.

2. The next sort of video fake is the film that is not quite yet a film. This is the pre-release director's cut, and it comes complete with time codes at the bottom of the screen. The visual and sound quality of these copies is better than the re-filmed fakes. As these fakes are based on initial audience previews, before a film is released, the ending in these videos can sometimes be different from the commercially released version, or contain scenes that do not make it to the cinema.

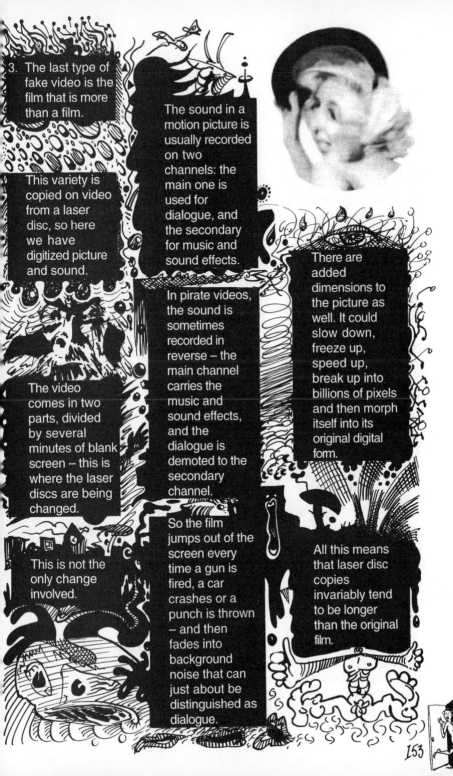

3. The last type of fake video is the film that is more than a film.

This variety is copied on video from a laser disc, so here we have digitized picture and sound.

The video comes in two parts, divided by several minutes of blank screen – this is where the laser discs are being changed.

This is not the only change involved.

The sound in a motion picture is usually recorded on two channels: the main one is used for dialogue, and the secondary for music and sound effects.

In pirate videos, the sound is sometimes recorded in reverse – the main channel carries the music and sound effects, and the dialogue is demoted to the secondary channel.

So the film jumps out of the screen every time a gun is fired, a car crashes or a punch is thrown – and then fades into background noise that can just about be distinguished as dialogue.

There are added dimensions to the picture as well. It could slow down, freeze up, speed up, break up into billions of pixels and then morph itself into its original digital form.

All this means that laser disc copies invariably tend to be longer than the original film.

153

New Technologies

Media technology is developing very rapidly. In the last decade alone, we have seen the emergence of desktop publishing, the Internet, cable, satellite and global television, digital and interactive television and CD-roms. We can expect new technologies to emerge at an ever-increasing rate.

The assumption that technological progress is inevitable and creates significant social change is called **technological determinism**. Not all new technologies are beneficial or indeed find favour with consumers. In spite of their predicted success, mini-discs, eight-track music cartridges and quadrophonic music sound systems failed to take off. We should thus be cautious when discussing the future of any new media technologies.

In general, new technologies elicit two varieties of opinion.

New technology leads to increasing access to information, and therefore new empowerment.

Multimedia companies will become increasingly powerful, leading to greater commercial exploitation and a wider gap between the information-rich and the information-poor.

The cultural optimists

The cultural pessimists

Cable and Satellite TV

Cable and satellite have different distribution systems, but also have several features in common. The main selling point is an increase in the number of channels available to the viewer. Sport, films, children's cartoons and pop music feature heavily on both. The trend is towards "narrowcasting" – focussing on specialist or niche audiences. Cable is better at this, as it can target local audiences, such as ethnic minorities.

At 24 billion dollars, News Corp. run by me, Rupert Murdoch, is one of the most powerful entities on the planet, printing and broadcasting in every populated continent except Africa.

Critics argue that this increase in channels does not benefit the viewer. They point out that the average amount of TV viewing has not increased – in fact, the 1990s saw a small decrease.

This means less investment in programme-making for terrestrial companies, which are being financially squeezed. Production quality may therefore be affected. The additional channels usually offer imported material which is endlessly recycled.

155

Digital and Interactive Television

Analogue television signals can be compressed into digital form, and it is therefore possible to put many more channels into a given frequency space. Interactive TV means that viewers can make choices above and beyond the simple channel changes that are now available.

Aaaaargh! That's just a bit too much interaction!

They could:

1. Select schedules, or a video on demand, by choosing from a menu.
2. Select programme options such as camera angles, action replays, etc.
3. Take part in games as a contestant, or take part in studio votes.
4. Do the shopping on-line.
5. E-mail and surf the Web through television.

The Web

The "World Wide Web" contains millions of "pages" of information stored on computers worldwide. These pages – containing text, pictures, animation, music, videos – can be accessed by means of a computer and a modem, and all the contents can be downloaded and stored. The Web has the potential to carry all forms of media, from newspapers to films. Indeed, films may soon be released directly on the Web.

Supporters of the Web argue that it opens up a new era of democratization by empowering ordinary people to produce and receive information and entertainment from all over the world.

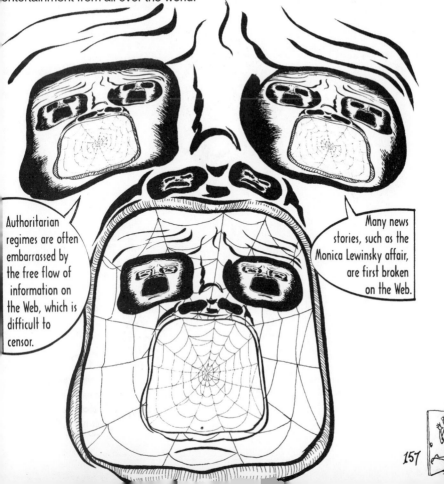

Criticisms of the Web

Critics point to the increasing use of pornography, and the fact that anti-democratic groups (such as neo-Nazis) have a strong presence on the Web. Even though there is an increase in information flow, many people still cannot access it. For example, South Africa is one of the fastest-growing Internet markets in the world, but less than one in 1,000 of its black population owns a phone. So the Web may lead to a division between information-rich and information-poor people within a society, as well as on a global level.

158

Ownership

The freedom of the press belongs to those who own one.

In all industrial markets there is a tendency for the bigger, more successful organizations to take over smaller companies. The media industry is no exception. Indeed, media conglomerates have expanded so rapidly that only a handful of companies now control most of the media output.

▲ Four Western news agencies supply 90% of the world's press, radio and television: Associated Press (AP), United Press International (UPI), Reuters, and Agence France-Presse (AFP). And over two-thirds of their correspondents are actually based in the West.

▲ Global television news is supplied by CNN, CNBC, BBC World Service TV, and, in some cases, various subsidiaries of News Corporation. During the 1991 Gulf War, both President George Bush and President Saddam Hussein relied on CNN for their news.

▲ Over half of all television programmes in Asia are imported from the West.

▲ Recorded music is controlled almost totally by five companies: PolyGram, Time Warner, Sony, EMI and Bertelsman.

▲ Global film production is dominated by the studios owned by: Disney, Time Warner, Viacom, Universal, Sony, PolyGram, MGM and News Corporation.

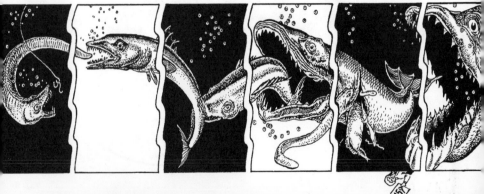

What is Synergy?

The term **synergy** is often used to describe the way in which one industry expands and diversifies to absorb related concerns in a ruthless attempt to maximize profits. A film like *The Last Action Hero* (1993) illustrates how synergy works in Hollywood.

The film was made by Columbia Pictures, which is owned by Sony Corporation.

The soundtrack came from CBS, which is also owned by Sony.

The film was screened in cinemas with digital sound systems made by Sony.

Sony then went on to make virtual reality games based on the movie, and also marketed related video games which work on Sony computer hardware.

To appreciate how much of the media market a single corporation may control, consider the companies owned by **Viacom**.

Television Networks

CBS MTV, VH1

Nickelodeon | Country Music TV

Nashville Network

Paramount Comedy Channel |

The Movie Channel

Film, TV Production

Paramount Pictures

Paramount Television

Spelling Television

King World Productions

Consumer Publishing

Simon & Schuster

cbs.sportsline

cbs.marketwatch

Other Operations

Infinity Networks (advertising group)

Blockbuster Video (retail chain)

Theme parks

MEGA-CONGLOMERATION

The accumulation of media companies in the hands of a few corporations has produced a great deal of concern and debate. In particular, Marxist writers have argued that ownership and control of the media enables media conglomerates to promote their own agenda – the political economy thesis. But the profit motive does not always lead to the upholding of dominant ideologies. Newspapers switch their political affiliations to boost circulation. The size of the budget of a Hollywood blockbuster does not always guarantee a profitable outcome. So economic forces can sometimes be more significant than ideological concerns.

MEDIA
IMPERIALISM

Blip. Blip. Blip.
This is the BBC World Service.
Now, "Matter for Debate", presented
by Walter MacMedia.*

Hello! Is the
Western media promoting cultural
imperialism? Is Western ownership of the media,
and the fact that the structure, content and distribution
of the media is dictated by the US and Europe,
exerting cultural pressures on the Third
World? This is the "Matter for
Debate" today.

* For it is he,
supplementing his
hard-earned millions by
moonlighting!

163

It is suggested that news flows only one way – from the West to the Third World. Here is an expert.

I'm a many-facetted cultural pundit, me.

Third World countries rely too heavily on Western news sources. The import of television programmes is destroying local film and television industries. Even the advertising is Western in origin and offers Western products and services. Most Third World countries are more vulnerable to advertising because of fewer regulatory controls. And multinational companies often side-step existing regulations by pretending to sell, for example, designer clothes, when they are actually selling cigarettes.

But does information merely flow from the West to other countries? This view, critics argue, is rather simplistic. Here is an expert with opposing views.

I'm the token W.A.S.P. in this book.

It is not true to say that the Third World is simply a passive recipient. There is, for example, a high level of regional exchange within the media, especially in Latin America and the Middle East. Also, countries like India and China originate most of their own media production – their film industries have a higher output than Hollywood. Indigenous material is familiar to them, and foreign imports, along with their cultures and beliefs, appear alien.

Soap opera is a media form that originated in 1940s American radio. It can survive cultural transfers across the globe only by changing radically. Soap operas in Brazil and India focus on local social issues. Even MTV had to adapt to survive. There are now American, European and Asian MTVs. In some areas, MTV failed due to a lack of understanding of this culture factor.

India is seen as a good example of how Western media can get it wrong. Star TV was launched in India in 1992, but only attracted 2% of an estimated 8 million viewers. But Zee TV, a real Hindi service, achieved 10% very quickly. Why? Because India is a complex society with over a billion people, over 300 languages, five main religions, a caste system, and extremes in wealth and education.

Star, which broadcast in English, attracted only a few younger, English-speaking people.

So the situation is not as simple as presented by the "media imperialism" model. Many experts now reject this model in its original form.

The question we should be asking is: how do global and local interact in contexts in which the media is just one of many sources of information?

CELEBRITY

Andy Warhol claimed...

Everyone is entitled to fifteen minutes of fame.

Celebrity, however, is a very different kind of phenomenon. The awarding of celebrity guarantees a lifetime of prominence, long after people can remember exactly why particular individuals are, or ever became, celebrities.

The 19th century was a time no less obsessed with celebrity than our own. It was money and social rank that conferred celebrity.

The social pages of newspapers reported the lifestyles of the rich and ennobled. What has changed in the 20th century is the social milieu that guarantees the attaining of celebrity. Wealth retains its privileges, but now inordinate prominence is given to people who work in the entertainment industry, the media and in sport.

Manufacturing Fame

The media are not only significant as the forum wherein celebrity is manufactured. They are also the prime consumer and employer of celebrity. As the budgetary constraints of making more television programmes for less money to occupy more channels and broadcast hours have become the norm, celebrity has become an incestuous, cannibalistic device of the medium.

The marquee value of a name is used to hook viewers, and very little celebrity can go a very long way.

Celebrity has become its own justification.

PRINCESS DIANA IN PURSUIT OF THE PAPPARAZZI

You only get one shot at fame.

Valerie Solonas, June 3, 1968 as she was being booked for the shooting of Andy Warhol

Any format or programme concept can be enhanced in its supposed ratings value by the inclusion of celebrities. The ultimate end of the syndrome is the *Larry King Live* show on CNN, in which celebrities not only talk about other celebrities but also put forward anodyne opinions on topical and important issues of our time.

The extreme of celebrity value is the Princess Diana phenomenon. Soap operas make fictional characters familiar by daily exposure. The phenomenal interest in the demise of a well-loved soap character has now been transferred to celebrities like Diana, who have become just as familiar by repeated coverage in the media. Reality mirroring artifice!

"Celebrity is a way in which meaning can be housed and categorized into something that provides a source and origin for meaning."

David Marshall, author of *Celebrity and Power* (1997)

THE PAPPARAZZI IN PURSUIT OF PRINCESS DIANA

Celebrity is like bad sex. Celebrity calls into existence the virtual aspect of our nature, its ability to become something different, something beyond what we expect of our species. The intercourse of public and celebrity draws attention to one thing that breaks the spell: the complete incompatibility of the public's desire with that of the celebrity. The sordid fact is that both jerk off on the other, but can never come together.

McKenzie Wark, Australian cultural critic and Lecturer in Media Studies, Macquarie University

THE FUTURE

How will the media change in the future?

The Future

In the near future, digital technology will revolutionize broadcasting. Consumer choice will proliferate, with countless new channels. But more will not necessarily mean better. And new technologies also have other drawbacks.

overload

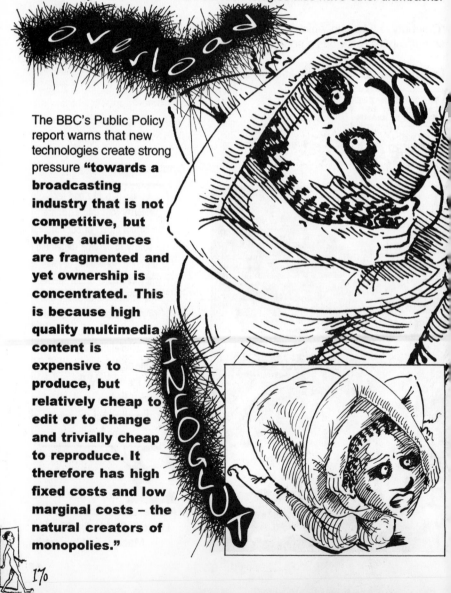

The BBC's Public Policy report warns that new technologies create strong pressure **"towards a broadcasting industry that is not competitive, but where audiences are fragmented and yet ownership is concentrated. This is because high quality multimedia content is expensive to produce, but relatively cheap to edit or to change and trivially cheap to reproduce. It therefore has high fixed costs and low marginal costs – the natural creators of monopolies."**

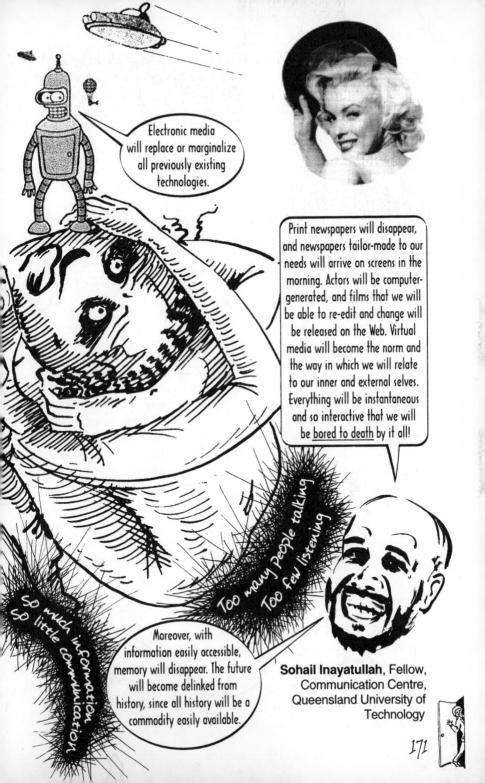

This does not mean that we will stop reading and writing, any more than we stopped talking when we learned how to read and write. But we will have to learn to communicate complex ideas with visual, electronic media. We will have to learn to "speed view", just as we learned how to "speed read".

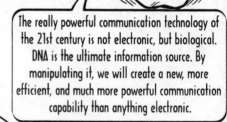

Jim Dator, Professor of Future Studies, University of Hawaii at Manoa, Honolulu

The really powerful communication technology of the 21st century is not electronic, but biological. DNA is the ultimate information source. By manipulating it, we will create a new, more efficient, and much more powerful communication capability than anything electronic.

What this means is that future media will help us connect with others at far deeper levels – we will become sensitive to other ways of knowing (multiculturalism), sensitive to nature (a green media), and sensitive to deeper levels of consciousness.

And so on into the defiant future!

Inayatullah

172

Reading List

You've read the classics, now here are the 100 best books on the media.

General
1. Brian Dutton, *The Media* (Harlow: Longman, 1997)
2. Tim O'Sullivan, Brian Dutton, Philip Rayner, *Studying the Media* (London: Arnold, 1998)
3. Stuart Price, *Media Studies* (Harlow: Longman, 1998)
4. Manuel Alvarado and John O. Thompson (eds), *The Media Reader* (London: BFI, 1990)
5. David Croteau and William Hoynes, *Media/Society: Industries, Images and Audiences* (Thousand Oaks, CA: Pine Forge Press, 1997)
6. Adam Briggs and Paul Cobley (eds), *The Media: An Introduction* (Harlow: Longman, 1998)
7. William Jawitz, *Understanding Mass Media*, 5th edn (Lincolnwood, IL: National Text Company, 1996)

Audience
8. Nicholas Abercrombie and Brian Longhurst, *Audiences* (London: Sage, 1998)
9. Glasgow University Media Group, *Bad News* (London: Routledge and Kegan Paul, 1980); *More Bad News* (Routledge and Kegan Paul, 1985)
10. Stuart Hall et al, *Policing the Crisis* (London: Macmillan, 1978)
11. Denis McQuail, *Mass Communication Theory* (Newbury Park, CA: Sage, 1987)
12. Paul Lazarsfeld et al, *The People's Choice* (New York: Columbia University Press, 1944)
13. Tamar Liebes and Elihu Katz, *The Export of Meaning* (Cambridge, Polity Press, 1993)
14. David Morley, *The Nationwide Audience* (London: BFI, 1980)

Television and News
15. Stuart Hood and Thalia Tabary-Peterssen, *On Television* (London: Pluto Press, 1997)
16. David McQueen, *Television: A Media Student's Guide* (London: Arnold, 1998)
17. Mike Wayne (ed.), *Dissident Voices: The Politics of Television and Cultural Change* (London: Pluto Press, 1998)
18. Mane Gillespie, *Television, Ethnicity and Cultural Change* (London: Routledge, 1995)
19. Brian McNair, *News and Journalism in the UK* (London: Routledge, 1999)

Film
20. Ashis Nandy (ed.), *The Secret Politics of Our Desires: Innocence, Culpability and Indian Popular Cinema* (London: Zed, 1998)
21. Ashish Rajadhyaksha and Paul Willemen, *Encyclopaedia of Indian Cinema* (London: BFI, 1994)
22. Bey Logan, *Hong Kong Action Cinema* (London: Titan Books, 1995)
23. Richard Shickel, *The Disney Version: The Life, Times, Art and Commerce of Walt Disney* (London: Pavilion, 1986)
24. Mark C. Carnes (ed.), *Past Imperfect: History According to the Movies* (London: Cassell, 1995)
25. Parker Tyler, *Early Classics of the Foreign Film* (London: Citadel Press, 1962)
26. Krishna Sen, *Indonesian Cinema* (London: Zed Books, 1994)
27. Michael T. Martin (ed.), *Cinemas of the Black Diaspora: Diversity, Dependence and Oppositionality* (Detroit: Wayne State University Press, 1995)
28. John Brosnan, *The Primal Screen: A History of Science Fiction Film* (London: Orbit, 1991)
29. Michael Wayne, *The Dialectics of Third Cinema* (London: Pluto Press, 2000)
30. Trinh T. Minh-Ha, *Framer Framed* (London: Routledge, 1992)
31. Ziauddin Sardar and Sean Cubitt (eds), *Aliens R Us: Cinema, Science Fiction and the Other* (London: Pluto Press, 2000)

Power and Ideology
32. Oliver Boyd-Barrett and Peter Braham (eds), *Media, Knowledge and Power* (Milton Keynes: Open University, 1987)
33. Edward S. Herman and Robert W. McChesney, *The Global Media: The New Missionaries of Corporate Capitalism* (London: Cassell, 1999)
34. Andrew Graham and Gavyn Davies, *Broadcasting, Society and Policy in the Multimedia Age* (Luton: University of Luton Press, 1997)

35. Jeff Cohen and Norman Solomon, *Adventures in Media Land: Behind the News and Beyond the Pundits* (Munroe, ME: Common Courage Press, 1993)
36. David Marshall, *Celebrity and Power* (Minneapolis: University of Minnesota Press, 1997)
37. Marshall McLuhan, *The Gutenberg Galaxy* (Toronto: University of Toronto Press, 1962); *Understanding Media* (New York: New American Library, 1964)
38. John Tomlinson, *Cultural Imperialism* (London: Pinter, 1994)
39. Ziauddin Sardar, *Postmodernism and the Other: The New Imperialism of Western Culture* (London: Pluto Press, 1998)
40. McKenzie Wark, *Celebrities, Culture and Cyberspace* (Annandale, NSW: Pluto Press, 1999)
41. Just World Trust, *Terrorising the Truth: The Shaping of Contemporary Images of Islam and Muslims in Media, Politics and Culture* (Penang: Just World Trust, 1997)
42. Ziauddin Sardar, *Orientalism* (Buckingham: Open University Press, 1999)

(continued on p. 222)

Aliens Write Book Shock!
From Our Own Correspondent

Two immigrants have shocked the establishment by writing a whole book! Writer **Ziauddin Sardar**, of indeterminate age, and illustrator **Borin Van Loon**, 48, have produced what they call "a comic study guide" on the media. "We came to Britain wearing only our own clothes", they say. "Were it not for this book, we would have continued to live in poverty and an artistic partnership would not have emerged", they add.

Sardar came to Britain 40 years ago from Dipalpur, a small Pakistani village. "My birth certificate was washed away in the monsoon rain, and so I have no idea when and if I was born", he says. Van Loon was born in a ramshackle barn on an East Anglian mountainside as Queen Elizabeth II assumed the throne. His grandfather remade history in Eindhoven by enrolling in an English as a Foreign Language class.

The unlikely pair claim that they have also written other books! "We have collaborated before on *Introducing Cultural Studies* and *Introducing Mathematics*", they say.

Sardar: in happier times
Sardar says he has edited more bus tickets then he can remember. But his experience, imagination and flair could not secure a plum job in the media. "Perhaps I have been overlooked because I speak with an 'Indian' accent and have a fine set of teeth", he says. He worked for the science journals *Nature* and *New Scientist* before joining London Weekend Television as a reporter. He now edits the monthly journal *Futures*, co-edits the quarterly journal *Third Text*, and writes regularly for the *New Statesman*.

Sardar says he would like to thank Gail Boxwell, Atif Imtiaz, Jan Mair and Merryl Wyn Davies for helping him put crumbs on his table.

THIS SPACE TO LET

See page 121

Van Loon: eraserhead
Van Loon, who has also illustrated *Darwin and Evolution*, *Genetics*, *Buddha*, *Sociology* and *Eastern Philosophy* in the *Introducing* series, claims to be a surrealist painter. "I have a rich and lubricious fantasy life", he says. One of his collage murals hangs in the Science Museum. He is now starting work on his first full-length feature, *From Exquisite Corpse To Pachuco Cadavre (Saucy Confessions Of An Ex-Librarian III)*.

Van Loon says he would like to thank God that he got this book finished on time.

Index

Adorno, T.W. 33-5
advertisers, pressure 93
advertising 107-11
  and children 12-15
  on television 125-6
  Third World 164
Althusser, Louis 55-6, 73
animation 103-4
audiences
  measuring 61-2
  situating 70
  specifying 62

Barthes, Roland
  38, 41, 73
BBC World Service 163
Bollywood 142-3
Broadcasting Standards
  Commission 12-15

canalization 23
capitalism 72
children
  and advertising 12-15
  and screen violence 26
Cohen, Stan 77-8
comics 101-2
commercial television 58
communication, lack of
  6-7
context 44
critical
  framework 65
  theory 33
Cubitt, Sean 5-11
cultivation theory 28
cultural
  indicators 28-9
  industry, media as 34
  products 16
culturalist studies 59

deconstruction 55
Derrida, Jacques 38, 55
discourse 49

editing
  films 130
  television 120-1
electronic media
  67, 171-2
  see also Internet
evolution, media studies
  21-38

film 16, 19, 127-47, 166
  as a metaphor 133-4
Foucault, Michel 38
Frankfurt School 33, 72

future of the media 170

genre 49
Gerbner, George 28-9
Gramsci, Antonio 59
gratifications theory 30-2

Hall, Stuart 59
hegemonic model 72-3
hegemony 59, 60
Hollywood 139-41
Hong Kong cinema 144
Horkheimer, Max 33-4

ideology 73
Indian film
  142-3, 145, 166
institutional studies 50
Internet 157-8
Iranian cinema 145

Katz, Elihu 30, 64

legislation and the media
  53
Lazarsfeld, Paul 22-4
Liebes, Tamar 64

magazines 20
Marcuse, Herbert 72
Margolis, Jonathan 9
Marshall, David 169
Marxism 33-6, 72
McQuail, Denis 31
media
  effects 26-9
  the future 170
  impact on voters
    23-5, 27
  needs 31
  ownership 159
  social influence 8
  term defined 6
  why study it? 3-5
mediation 48
metaphor 45
metonymy 46
monopolization 23
myth 73

narrative 47
news 89-100
newspapers 20, 61

paradigm 44
pluralistic model 74
Policing the Crisis 59
political economy 57-8
print media 36-7

professionals in media
  51-4
propaganda 13-14
public
  opinion 24-5
  service broadcasting
    124-6

racist stereotypes 79-81
radio 63, 105-6
ratings 62-3
reality, constructing 78
referential framework 65
representation, media
  71-88
research 22-32

Saussure, F. de 38, 39
school, media studies 15
screen violence 26
semiology 38-49, 56
  in film 127
signs 43
  see also semiology
soap operas 165, 168
stereotypes 75-88, 137
structuralism 55-8
studies 22-9, 64-7,
  68-9
  see also culturalist
  studies
supplementation 23
symbol 43
synergy 160-2
syntagm 44

technological determinism
  154
television 18, 112-28
  advertising on 125-6
  cable/satellite 154-5
  commercial 58
  Dallas study 64-7
  digital/interactive 156
  Nationwide study 68-9
texts, types of 44

uses and gratifications
  theory 30-2

video 148-53
Videography 5
violence on TV 26, 29
voting habits 24

war reporting 97, 99-100
women
  films 138
  stereotypes 82-8